# A Vindication of th Sabbath and the Commandments of God

## With a Further History of God's Peculiar People from 1847-1848

Joseph Bates

**Alpha Editions**

This edition published in 2024

ISBN : 9789362998736

Design and Setting By
**Alpha Editions**
www.alphaedis.com
Email - info@alphaedis.com

As per information held with us this book is in Public Domain.
This book is a reproduction of an important historical work. Alpha Editions uses the
best technology to reproduce historical work in the same manner it was first
published to preserve its original nature. Any marks or number seen are left
intentionally to preserve its true form.

# Contents

# Preface.

I DEDICATE to you the following pages, with my continued prayers to God, through our Great High Priest and coming King, that they may, in connection with God's Holy Word and guidance of the Divine Spirit, enable you more clearly to discover the deceptive arts of the Devil, and the agents he is employing in these last days, to betray and ensnare you in his (almost) innumerable and complicated variety of sins and snares; and see your true position *just here* under the HIGH LANDS of IMMORTALITY! Do not forget, while seeking to understand the Scriptures with a simple and honest desire to live *here* by every word of God, to read again and again the warning that God in his infinite mercy gave to Jesus more than fifty years after his glorious resurrection and triumphant ascension to his Father's seat in his Sanctuary in the heaven of heavens; and he sent it by his angel, who presented it before John in holy vision, recorded in his Rev. xii: 13 and 17, and in xvi. chapter, first part of the 13th, and 14th and 15th verses. You will see the opening developement of these very things in the work before you. None will fully realize them but those who are keeping *all* of the Commandments of God, especially his Holy Seventh-day Sabbath. Without fear of contradiction here or hereafter before the great WHITE THRONE, I tell you there is not an Advent paper (that I have heard of) published in the land, that is leading to the kingdom. I do not say but what they publish many truths; but their heretical doctrines will, if followed, never, no never, lead you to God! And as you pass along through these peace and safety *valves* in your prophetical history, watching and anxiously waiting for God to give the fourth sign of the coming of Jesus by shaking the heavens and earth, the sea and all nations, and give you the *time* of Jesus' coming, you will more clearly discover the widening track these advocates are pursuing with almost to a *unit* every professed advent minister in their train. You will also see that the *Waymarks* and high heaps in your pathway, *past and present*, are the only sure earthly guides to the peaceful haven of eternal rest. From my watch-tower I have discovered and pointed out to you some of the devouring WOLVES in sheep's clothing. Let us avoid them, and live prayerful, humble and watchful, for more will yet be seen, and perhaps start right out of your midst!

As I am unable to pay the Printer, your means—as God has given you ability—will be needed. I trust that God's true children are ready.

Fairhaven, Mass. Jan. 1848.
J. B.

# The Sabbath Controversy.

Once more I feel constrained to speak in vindication of the Sabbath of the Lord our God. I have been privileged to read about all the articles which have appeared in the BIBLE ADVOCATE, both for and against the Seventh-day Sabbath, for about four months past; and occasionally a thrust and a challenge from the Advent Harbinger, declaring that the law of God was abolished more than eighteen hundred years ago, and that we have since that time been under grace. The most that I have feared in this controversy was, that it would not be continued long enough to bring out the whole truth, to the utter confusion and dismay of these professed Second Advent Sabbath breakers. One trait in their characters is now pretty clearly developed, that is—they are Sabbath haters! The law of God is nicknamed by them, the "Jewish Ritual," the "Jewish Sabbath," the "Sabbath of the old Jews," &c. &c., thus virtually showing up their characters in these perilous times, according to Paul, as covenant breakers, boasters, proud, blasphemers, denying the righteous law of God, and yet professing to believe the whole word of God. "As Jannes and Jambres withstood Moses" so do some of these leading men resist the truth. "A wonderful and horrible thing is committed in the land, the prophets prophecy falsely and the priests bear rule by their means, and my people love to have it so; and what will ye do in the end thereof?" Answer—"The soul that sinneth, it shall die." I think it is becoming very evident that they are fulfilling Rev. xii: 17, and xvi: 13, first clause. None others so likely to deceive as these, because of their position in the near coming of the Saviour. It amounts to almost an impossibility to get *their* definition of the *Law and Commandments*. One class will tell you that the old and new testaments are the Word and Commandments of God. A second will tell you that the new testament contains all the commandments and teachings that are now required of us. I was informed of a company of professed advent believers, not thirty miles from this, having become so alarmed or tenacious, that they would not carry the old testament with them to meeting on the first day. There was nothing in it, however, that they feared but the commandment to keep the Seventh-day Sabbath. A third class will tell you that baptism, the Lord's Supper, washing one another's feet, holy greeting, and all the commands which are given, are commandments. Joseph Marsh, editor of the Advent Harbinger, says we are not under the law (of Moses) but under the law of grace, the new testament. Now the Apostle James has given us a test which will utterly confound all such unscriptural arguments, viz.: "Whosoever shall keep the whole law but shall fail with respect to one precept hath been guilty of all."—[*Macknight's trans.*] Now to make it still plainer for us, he says, "For he who commanded do not commit adultery, hath commanded also, do not kill. Now if thou commit not adultery, *but killest*, thou hast become a transgressor of the law." Now I ask in all candor which of these *five* are right? You answer, James, the inspired one. Well, does he justify either of the other four? You answer no, for he has directed us to the tables of stone, the ten commandments in the law, recorded in Exodus xx: 1-17. This is the true source. Is it doubted? Then here is the testimony of Jesus in Matt. v: 17-19. Now read the 21st and 27th verses— the very same ones James has quoted. See also the 33d verse, the third precept. There are several others if required, but surely these two are clear. Certainly no one will doubt from the above testimony but what the ten commandments in the decalogue are all and the only ones that man is required to keep, with the exception of the new one in John xiii: 34, given for the church of Christ. But J. Marsh says, it is clear that all the ten commandments in the decalogue were abolished at the crucifixion of Christ. So says every one that takes this stand, and they quote for proof 2d Col. 14-17. But it happens very unfortunately for them all that James saw his master crucified and his testimony is dated A.D. 60, about twenty-nine years beyond their point of time, and shows us that the commandments were as much enforced then and ever would be, as they were when his master was crucified twenty-nine years before. Now I say that this testimony pointedly and positively condemns them and will condemn them at the judgment. For proof of this I appeal to the teachings of our Lord Jesus Christ, what we must do to be saved, "*If thou wilt enter into life, keep the commandments.*" But some will say James called it the law, therefore you must so expound it. I will let God and Jesus do that: God says positively that the keeping of the Seventh-day Sabbath is my *commandment and my law.* Exod. xvi: 28, 29. So he has in other places taught us respecting the whole decalogue, and so in like manner does Jesus. Read the same question and answer recorded in Luke x: 25-28: "WHAT SHALL I DO TO INHERIT ETERNAL LIFE?" Jesus asks him what is written in the LAW. He repeats the words of Jesus recorded in Matt. xxii: 36-40, or, in 37-39th verses. "*And* (Jesus) *said unto him, thou hast answered* RIGHT *this do and* THOU SHALT LIVE." Now, if you want it still clearer, read Matt v: 17-19. Law and commandments are here too, synonymous: "Whosoever therefore shall break one of these least [*laws*] commandments, and shall teach men so, shall be in no esteem in the reign of heaven, but whosoever shall *practice* and teach them shall be highly esteemed in the reign of heaven."—[*Campbell trans.*] That he is speaking of the law of commandments in the decalogue is positive and clear from the 21st, 27th and 33d verses. That he means the whole, is also clear from this and the above quotations in Matt. xxii. and Luke x. Now if the keeping of the commandments will secure us eternal life, and the violation of them render us of no esteem in the reign of heaven, how can those enter there who do not keep them, and especially such ones as Joseph Marsh and his adherents, who are teaching the world that there are no commandments, and are endeavoring to dissuade and discourage and reproach all of God's honest children, who are striving to be highly esteemed in the reign of heaven. Does not the Saviour's language as clearly apply to them now as it did when he was permanently establishing and confirming this covenant, the law and commandments of God, "putting them into our minds and writing them on our hearts." viz.: "Why do ye also transgress the commandments of God by *your* tradition? Ye hypocrites, well did Esaias prophecy of you saying, this people draweth nigh unto me with their mouth, and honoreth me with their lips," [They are advocating his speedy coming to judge the world.] "but their heart is far from me. But *in vain* they do worship me *teaching* for *doctrines the commandments of men.*" Oh, but say some, we believe that the commandments are as valid now as they ever were. Why do you then constantly and perseveringly reject, scoff at, and sneeringly deride, and denounce, those that are as honest as you are, while they are endeavoring to keep the fourth commandment just as God had directed them? When you have been so repeatedly shown by their writings, drawn from the clear word that the fourth commandment is not abolished and *never* has undergone any change more than the other nine, and that there is no other weekly sabbath recorded or intimated in the old and new testaments. If you will follow such downright infidelity as is taught in *all* the second advent papers respecting God's holy sabbath, and still continue to stigmatize the holy law of God, how can you expect to be treated otherwise than the rebellious house of Israel, and be made to feel in a very little while from this, all the horrors of a guilty conscience, urging you to do that which you now detest and abhor: even to come and bow at the feet of these very despised—as you are now disposed to term them—"*door shutters,*" "*mystery folks,*" "*Judaizers,*" "*feet washers,*" "*deluded fanatics,*" *&c. &c.* See Isa. xlix: 23, and lx: 14; Rev. iii: 9. Here your characters are delineated. You say no, these mean the nominal church. It is not so. *They* have rejected the message of the second advent. And *you* since that time (1814) have rejected the word of God. Our testimony will not be rejected when called for that you with us left them with all their creeds and confessions of faith and professed to take the whole word of God for our rule of faith and practice. This then is your clear position, even while opposing the commandments of God. If you ask why I speak in such positive terms about or concerning the commandments of God, allow me to cite you to our history, Rev. xiv: 12. Is not this positive proof?

Also in xii: 17. Do you not read your own characters as described above, on the remnant of the last end? and are not these individuals who enter the gates of the city the same remnant that are at last saved by keeping the commandments? xxii: 14. Does not the 15th verse describe those who are left out, "and whosoever loveth and maketh a *lie.*" How perfectly this compares with what I quoted above, Rev. iii: 9. See also 1st John ii: 4. "He that saith I know him and keep not his commandments is a LIAR and the *truth* is not in him." You will possibly say the three texts which I have quoted in Rev. xii., xiv. and xxii., have no reference to the Sabbath. When I come to treat on the xiv. of Rev. I will look at this point. But allow me to state here, that the first three commandments in the decalogue have never been a subject of dispute (*separately*) in Christendom, while the fourth *has* been for fifteen hundred years. We know positively that this is true in our second advent experience. Therefore it is plain that by keeping the fourth commandment or the seventh-day Sabbath as it stands recorded, and in the very time too in our history, we are clearly fulfilling the prophecy, viz.: "Here is the patience of the saints, here are they that keep the commandments of God and the faith of Jesus." Allow me to state my conviction here with reference to the great mass of advent believers especially, that if they could quietly dispose of the seventh-day Sabbath and sink it with the Jewish rituals, then they would never raise their voice against the other nine commandments of God. This, then, is the evident reason why they are wielding their puny weapons to smite down the only foundation that upholds the old and new testament. It would be much easier work for them to stop the raging of the hurricane. God has them in derision, he will laugh them to scorn. But I must pass to the examination of this subject, as I intimated in the beginning.

IS THE FIRST DAY OF THE WEEK THE SEVENTH?

Before entering upon this subject, it will be proper for me to state, that some time last August the editor of the Bible Advocate, being pressed by his brethren to open his columns for the discussion of the Sabbath question, rather reluctantly complied, by first giving his views against it. He stated that he should first give C. Stowe's view, in the affirmative, covering the whole ground, and then the view of some other writer in the negative, before he published any thing more on the other side, and so on. Sister Stowe's piece, accompanied by the views of the editor, appeared in the B. A., Sept. 2d, 1847. C. Stowe sent the editor two articles, as she says. The editor saw proper to publish her second article and withhold the first, for purposes best known to himself. Perhaps it was considered objectionable, as the editor of the Advent Harbinger had refused to publish it for her. So for some reason or other, only part of the ground was covered, and not one candid objection or examination offered to her second, except by a certain character, who, apparently, was ashamed to have his real name known among honest seekers for the truth. So far as the subject has advanced, J. Croffut, of N. Y. city, J. B. Cook, of New Bedford, Mass. and A. Carpender, of Sutton, Vt. have spoken in the affirmative. The negative is advocated by the editor, Joseph Turner and Barnabas, and perhaps two others; besides what has been teeming from the Advent Harbinger, in the negative. Now, I do not reexamine Turner and Barnabas, because they have not been ably replied to by J. Croffut, J. B. Cook and C. Stowe of N. H., but because I see the necessity of taking up the subject in a different form, without being restricted, as all generally are, who write for papers. Another important point which governs me, is, that all the little flock may understand the true bearings of the subject, for there are undoubtedly a great many that do not see the Bible Advocate, and because I felt like taking a part in this great subject, in which I feel deeply interested, and I see from the commencement that I was excluded from that paper, by the statement that C. Stowe would cover the whole ground in the affirmative. I furthermore perceived there were additional objections to their unscriptural views, which continued to be presented to my mind.

JOSEPH TURNER in attempting to prove that Sunday, the first day of the week is the seventh day of the week, and therefore the proper Sabbath, has failed to make out his case. His proposed foundation is from Matt. xii: 39, 40. "But he answered and said unto them, an evil and adulterous generation seeketh after a sign, and there shall no sign be given to it, but the sign of the prophet Jonas, for as Jonas was three days and three nights in the whale's belly, so shall the son of man be three days and three nights in the heart of the earth." He says, "to rear the temple of this body in three days, or to remain in the heart of the earth three nights and to rise the *third* day was, according to the above scripture, to be a sign. I will now prove by Christ and his disciples that this sign was literally given, and that he arose, not the second, but *third* early in the morning." This statement is not true. The above scripture states *three* days, and not as you say you will now prove *in* three days. If it proves any thing, it proves three whole days, and then of course the Saviour would rise on the fourth day. This, according to your mode of calculating, would make the seventh day come on Monday. If you want the third day, or within three days, why not take as many as you need for your argument, from the eighteen other texts, and not take this isolated one, and then pervert it, as you have done. The only object that I can see, in your perversion of the text, is to prove, as you say, that Jesus was three nights in the heart of the earth, viz.: Friday night, one; Saturday night, two, and Sabbath night, three. You say, "that Christ was actually raised the *third* day and not the second, as tradition holds it." I am not aware of any such tradition. That would be perverting the whole eighteen texts instead of the one you have done. But that he was raised the third day, and that third day was the first of the week, is the joint testimony of the four evangelists, Matt. xxviii: 1; Mark xvi: 2; Luke xxiv: 1; John xx: 1. But let us see how you have obtained these *three* nights as stated above, which, as you say, "proves triumphantly that 'OUR SABBATH' is the seventh day." First read the second paragraph in your P. S., where you have attempted to pervert the plain and clear testimony of Luke, in chap. xxiii: 54, 56. Here you stated one scriptural fact: That the Sabbath always commenced at evening. "From evening to evening shall you celebrate your Sabbath."

Then, as a most natural consequence, the next day would begin where the Sabbath ended, and so of every other day thenceforward, or chaos and confusion would follow. This also perfectly agrees with God's manner of commencing time at the creation: "The evening (first,) and the morning is the first day," &c. Now as you have shown that Friday was the first day of the crucifixion and that it was so far spent and passed away at the time our Lord was buried, that the women could not have got home and prepared spices, (which probably was not more than twenty minutes labor,) before the next day began. How, and by what authority do you claim Friday night? Does Friday night come after twenty-four hours of that day are spent? You see how difficult God makes the way of transgressors. You may reply that you made a mistake. Will you allow me to tell you where your mistake commenced on this subject. If I am not very much mistaken it was when you gave up keeping the true seventh day, the only historical, chronological or biblical day of the week ever given to man. Well, you may say, I have made some converts. True—but they are also deceived, and many very likely rejoicing in it like D. B. WYATT, who seems to have swallowed the whole, and is endeavoring, with the assistance of the Advent Harbinger, (although they are at antipodes respecting the commandments of God,) to spread the glad tidings far and wide. This editor is in no wise particular about men and measures to accomplish his Jesuitical purpose, to annihilate the very foundation and superstructure of the Bible, "the commandments of God." Matt. xxii: 40. This wonderful piece of Advent intelligence is recorded in the same paper with D. B. Wyatt's, Sept 9, 1847. See also April 28, page 38. Let it be well understood here also, that this man and J. V. Himes, editor of the Advent Herald, are the two, and only two, editors and papers in this country, which William Miller of Lowhampton, N. Y. recommends to give the light on the second Advent. The meat in due season.

Your erroneous doctrine is heartily welcomed by some here, and many I understand in New Bedford, and very likely many in other places. Yes, I have heard of it away on the Lakes. I was told by one the other day who had backslidden like yourself, that it was the best argument he had yet seen. Now if you undertake to rectify your mistake, it is possible you may destroy all their joy, until some one presents another error—for the truth, it seems, they are determined not to have. Again, you say, "let my brethren remember that the law of Moses, made the first day of the feast of the passover, a sabbath in which no work should be done; this was the Sabbath that drew on. Moreover, I will here prove that the next day following the crucifixion, was not the Sabbath of the Lord, which the Jews at that time kept.—See Luke xxiii: 54." Now, I say if you will read the next two verses, 55 and 56, which are connected with 54, it will positively contradict your assertion, for it proves that they did keep the next day as the Sabbath, according to the commandment, and the seventh-day Sabbath was and is, the only Sabbath commandment in the whole bible. You pass this over and cite us to Matt xxvii: 62, 64, and base your whole proof on *inference*. It is this, that the Jews were so strict and pious in the observance of the Sabbath that they would not have gone to Pilate on that day to have asked him to set a watch over the body of Jesus, if it had been the Sabbath, because it would be an important fact to record against them. "How easy to have said in this record that the Jews on the Sabbath," &c. Yes sir, it would have been just as easy for *your* purpose, to have said in this record also, that "OUR SABBATH *is the Seventh day*." Then probably you would not have to answer for the sin which you have in these instances, knowingly committed. Besides this, you must have calculated largely on the credulity of your readers, to suppose that *all* of them would swallow such absurdities. As that men, who had just committed one of the most aggravating crimes ever recorded in the annals of history, in barbarously and cruelly murdering the son of the living God, should then for fear of having it recorded against them as touching the purity of their motives that they had violated the holy Sabbath of God by calling on the Governor, on the Sabbath of the Lord God, to set a watch over their victim, for fear that some of his disciples would come and steal him away, and thus openly expose them to the scorn of the world. This is your proof why the next day after the crucifixion could not be the Sabbath. How unfortunate and trying it must be to you, who, after being so highly extalled by your hearers in New Bedford, Fairhaven, &c., for your clear and plain Holy Ghost living and preaching, to have to flee to such mean subterfuges to establish a position to justify your backsliding from the plain and positive texts which stand right in your way.

Respecting your text in Matt. xii: 40. If you made use of it as it stands, it would positively prove the resurrection to be on the closing hours of Monday, between 3 and 6 P.M. and not in the morning, as every where recorded. So then, to fulfill your text to the very extent, and have the resurrection in the morning, it must be on Tuesday morning, for, Monday morning would bring you twelve hours too soon, only two and a half days instead of three. This would make *your* Sabbath, as you exultingly claim it for your adherents, come on Monday; that is, by your new mode of establishing the Sabbath. And then D. B. Wyatt, if he followed your strange view, would have to recall his address to his brethren and change the time of celebrating the Lord's Supper on Monday evening, and have it on Tuesday. I presume the editor of the Harbinger would have no objections to the alteration, provided Mr. W. was satisfied.

I know it is stated that Jonas was three days and three nights in the whale's belly. I know of no way to prove it but by the recorded time that our Lord was in the earth. You see that Matthew says *as he was* three days, &c. Now for the proof of how long *he was there*. First testimony—his disciples, Luke xxiv: 21-23. Second testimony—Angels, v: 7. Third testimony—Jesus himself, 46 v. "Thus it behoved Christ to suffer and to rise from the dead the *third* day." This testimony, be it remembered, was given a few hours after the resurrection, on the same day. Here then is the proof of what Jesus had before asserted, recorded ten times by the evangelist, and once by Paul; 1st Cor. xv: 4; Matt. xvi: 21; xvii: 23; xx: 19; Mark ix: 31; x: 34 and viii: 31;[1] Luke ix: 22; xiii: 32; xviii: 33; John ii: 19. And five times by his accusers, Matt. xxvi: 61; xxviii: 40 and 63; Mark xiv: 58; xv: 29. Every one of these eighteen texts records the resurrection *in* three, some of them *within* three days; and not a syllable about *nights*. The one in Matt xii: 40, says three days and three nights, referring to Jonas, as above. Now I ask, shall we take this one isolated text, out of the harmony of the whole eighteen, *and then pervert it*, to prove that some how or other the world have lost one day, and therefore the first day of the week is the seventh. We all know that our judgment always rests on the majority or weight of evidence. Here then we have seven to one besides the testimony of Jesus himself after his resurrection, that he arose the *third* day, and clearly demonstrating that he did not lie there three days and three nights, and proving, to my judgment, that Jonas was also delivered the third day. See other scripture rules, Esther iv: 16, 17, and v: 1. Here the Jews were to fast three days, but Esther ended it the *third*. See also 1st Kings, xx: 29, the seven days ended on the seventh. Also, Gen. xvii: 12, eight days. Lev. xii: 3, shows the eighth the same. Thus we see that the testimony of Jesus is clear.

It is clear to my mind that the Lord Jesus was not at furthest, more than thirty-eight hours in the tomb, and yet he was there, according to scripture proof, a part of Friday, the sixth day, *all* of the seventh day, Sabbath, and a part of Sunday, the first day, which last was the third day. Proof, Luke xxiii: 54-56. "And that day was the preparation and the Sabbath drew on." Mark this, that the preparation had come, and they were drawing to the Sabbath. *See here*, the preparation was always on the day of the Passover, the fourteenth of the first month. The feast day was the fifteenth, the next day. Let Moses give the time: "And ye shall keep it up [the Lamb] until the fourteenth day of the same month, and the whole assembly of the congregation of Israel shall kill it in the evening." Exo. xii: 6. The original—see margin—reads *between the two evenings*. See the same in Num. xxviii: 4,—practiced and carried out even to lighting the lamps in the tabernacle. Exo. xxx: 8.

Now our blessed Lord expired on the cross at the very time that this preparation always took place for 1670 years before, namely, the ninth hour, (Matt. xxvii, and Mark xv,) three o'clock in the afternoon. Then between the two evenings is just three hours, from 3 to 6 P. M. Keep this clear in mind and you will clearly understand how the disciples could have three hours from the death of their master to see him put in the tomb, to have gone and "bought sweet spices." (Mark xvi: 1,) and be ready to keep the Sabbath according to the commandment, (please read it in Exo. xx: 8-11,) as stated in Luke xxiii: 54-56. You will understand Mark xv: 42, "Now when the even was come because it was the preparation, *that is the day before the Sabbath*," that it was the ninth hour, or 3 P.M. Here the preparation goes on for three hours, until the Sabbath commenced. You see he says this was the day before the Sabbath, and when the Sabbath was passed, early in the morning of the first day, they found he had arisen. Mark xvi. Here then is the three days: The day before the Sabbath he was entombed, between the hours of 3 and 6 P.M., and the day after the Sabbath, the first day of the week, he arose. As J. B. Cook says, I can conceive of nothing more definite. Whitby and Scott say, "It is a received rule among the Jews that a part of a day is put for a whole day." And so, let me add, it is with the commercial nations of the earth. Every bill, or note, or deed, counts the day of its date and the day of its extinguishment. For instance, the transaction of an interest note takes place at half past 11 o'clock in the evening of the first day of January, 1847, and the interest is cast to the first day of January, 1848, the demand for it would be valid if called for at 30 minutes A. M. after midnight. Both of these dates are counted days in this and all other kinds of business transactions, as we reckon time. And I say it is impossible for any rational being to understand it in any other way. When one day ends the next begins, and so I have amply shown is the bible rule. Then, according to the testimony adduced, if the Saviour was placed in the tomb any where between the hours of 3 and 6 o'clock P. M. on Friday, then I say that day was as much counted for one, as the day on which he arose; and no man, not even J. Turner, undertakes to say that it was more than a part of a day. That this work of preparation was all accomplished before the Sabbath came, is perfectly clear from the two passages already quoted in Luke and Mark. See also John xix: 31. Here then the antetype agrees perfectly with the type, all the preparation work accomplished between the hours of three and six in the evening, called between the two evenings. Much also has been said about the next day, the fifteenth being a Jewish festival Sabbath, and therefore God's seventh-day Sabbath could not possibly be until the day after. Just as well might it be asserted when our fourth of July happens to fall on Sunday, that it could not be Sunday, because it was the anniversary of our independence, but the next day would be Sunday. This explains all the difficulty. This feast day of theirs always following the Passover day, happened this year to come on God's holy Sabbath day, hence the peculiar expression of John, "for that Sabbath was an high day." God's instruction to Moses respecting all the feast days is right to the point, "*Every thing upon his day.*" Lev. xxiii: 37. You see there is no provision to defer the Sabbath festivals whenever they happened on the Sabbath of the Lord our God.

Now I think the above Scriptures do clearly and incontrovertibly establish the resurrection to have been on Sunday morning, the first day of the week, and the day before, on which the Saviour rested in the tomb and his disciples in the city of Jerusalem, was the seventh day of the week, the Sabbath of the Lord our God, according to the commandment; and the day before that, viz. on Friday, he was crucified and buried. This clearly overthrows your unscriptural arguments to establish the first day of the week for the seventh-day Sabbath.

I have gone much further into this argument than I should, had I not have heard and seen the incalculable mischief that was being accomplished by the spread of such an argument; from one too, who is looked upon by those not personally acquainted with him as an ambassador, fully approved of God; a pillar in the church of these last days; one who is fully competent to preach and take the lead in camp-meetings, &c. &c. And still I feel there is a duty devolving upon me, which I ought not to shrink from, notwithstanding his high profession, and being fostered, and upheld as a brother beloved, by the Advent papers.

It is that since the winter of 1845, you have, by your deceptive arts, and false expositions of God's Word, taught and practiced ridiculous things in the churches, such as God never has, nor ever will approve. Your confession last spring in the Boston Conference seemed more like justifying and exalting yourself from your debased and fallen condition, than a bible confession, which says, "confess your faults one to another." But you perceived, I suppose with others, that it had become fashionable to confess the monstrous errors in our past experience in the advent doctrine to those who had drawn back and organized under the Laodocean state of the church. And also, that J. Marsh of Rochester, and others from different places, were distinguishing themselves by their wonderful confessions; therefore you also confessed how sorry you were for the mischief (or injury) that you had done the cause of God by writing and preaching the doctrine of *shut door* and *Bridegroom come.* Here you attempted to put down and destroy two of the most important and prominent truths according to the types and new testament teaching, with our history in the past, that is connected with the "twenty-three hundred days," and "cleansing of, or vindicating the sanctuary"; and use them as a scape goat to carry off and hide your unholy and iniquitous practices from their view. Why not confess that after you and A. Hale had published this clear scriptural view, that you had been so positive that you were right in your position, that at one of your meeting places in Portsmouth, N. H., you declared that you was ready to seal it with your own heart's blood, and that the appointment which you afterwards made to meet at Richard Walker's, if not, you would state the reason by writing, had been utterly disregarded, although you had passed through there several times. Why not confess with contrition your unscriptural teachings and practices? And lastly, why not inform your listening audience of the wonderful discovery and proficiency which you had made during that time, in the growing science of your predecessors, "Jannes and Jambres?" and what a loving drawing and wonderful effect this mesmeric influence produced on some of the dear sisters! You was aware that such kind of satanic practices would not go down with your hearers, therefore you withheld it probably for a more convenient season. The response from heaven to this confession (I think) is long since recorded by a servant of the Lord. Isa. i: 10-15. Since you began to preach in New Bedford, where it was said such a wonderful revival was following your preaching and practice, that some in Fairhaven were looked upon as sinners, because they would not believe that you were filled with the Holy Ghost. Here in New Bedford, I am told, that in reply to some of these charges: that you had studied or looked into the subject of mesmerism that you might ascertain the cause, or meaning, of the delusions practiced by the advent people. I think that by comparing dates, it may pretty clearly be known that this is one of the first and principal causes of the state of things now among many in Maine, especially where your influence was felt. In the course of this conversation you stated something else, which you will remember, and for fear, or something else, that it would not be believed, you said you could prove it by certain persons whom you named. I have since ascertained that these persons neither *know*, nor have ever *known*, or *have intimated any such thing*. Now, I ask, how much your confessions are worth in Boston or any where else. In the name of my Master, I here warn the little flock to beware of your ungodly teaching.

Since answering your argument on the first day for the seventh, I see by the Advocate of Dec. 16th, your exulting reply to J. B. Cook. Because he has not met every point of your twisted, sophistical argument, you now think it will stand forever. You say "The position *I* have taken will stand the onset of *all* while the eternal rock of inspiration stands secure; hence with confidence calm as heaven, I take my pen to reply," &c. We read that "the Devils believe and tremble," while this wonderful man is *calm* as *heaven*, because he thinks he has gained one day since the crucifixion, which would destroy the law of God, the fourth commandment, when in fact he has only stole six or eight hours. Perhaps he will try to borrow or take the balance in the forthcoming articles which he promises. And here he says again, "*the matter shall* REST *without a* REVIEW ON EITHER SIDE"!! "Vanity of vanities, saith the preacher!" Will God's word forever remain unvindicated, because of your veto? Your one mistake that I have shown, proves your infallibility. Let me repeat it in connection: In your text, Matt. xii: 39, 40, it states three days and three nights. This itself overthrows the whole of your argument—for three days are just as long as three nights. See how it will work by *your* rule: Jesus entombed just about 6 P.M. on Friday. Now count—Friday evening, one night; Saturday evening, two nights; Sunday evening, three nights. Now for the days: Saturday, one; Sunday, two; and Monday three. But to make it three, the resurrection must be on Monday evening, at 6 o'clock, and the scripture says he arose in the  morning! Then if you wait until Tuesday morning, you make it just three and a half days and four nights, and *your* Sabbath commences on Monday. But if you say it must be Monday morning, then you have but two days and twelve hours. You say this would be the third day, just as I say— true, but this text says "three days." Besides, you say in your second article, "some have been so *vain* on this point as to count the day of the crucifixion, one; the next day, one; and then the morning while it was yet dark, one; and therefore the third day. *This is almost wicked.* Does not Jesus Christ in whose word we trust—say three *nights?*" Yes, sir, and does he not as expressly say three *days,* too? If we are almost wicked in counting, as *you* say, then all the evangelists were, Mark and Luke especially. I say there is no other rule but the one you call us *vain* for using. If it is almost wicked to count a part of the first day, for one day, by what authority do you count a part of the last day, for one day? The scripture no where says, *two* days, and *three* nights.

And then as I have shown where you borrowed a part of a night, by counting Friday night for one of your three nights, when you insisted upon it that it was past, because the disciples had no time left of Friday to even prepare their spices. Did you not see that if you claimed six hours of Friday, to break the scriptures, that the disciples would have just as much time to prepare for the Sabbath? How is it that you do not understand what the angel Gabriel said should be in the last days: "But the wicked shall do wickedly, and none of the wicked shall understand." I really hope no one will be troubled with your forthcoming article. It would be far easier for you to shovel the Alleghany mountains into Lake Ontario than to attempt to gain one day, or prove that we have lost one.

Your threat about the fallacy of history, and what you will do about it, is also vain; yet, if you could do so, the bible is a sufficient rule in this case. You have therefore made but two and a half days and two nights, and work it which way you will, you will fail. You cannot destroy the validity of the other eighteen texts.

It is clear that the Jewish feasts always occurred when they fell on the Sabbath of the Lord. Lev. xxiii: 37, last cl.

# Barnabas Against The Sabbath.

Barnabas would fain have the world believe that God has made one law which man could never keep without leading him into bondage. He says, "Sister Stowe, nor any others of like faith pretends to keep the seventh-day according to the commandment, that reads, 'thou shalt not do any work.' Exo. xx: 10. 'Let no man go out of his place on the seventh day.' There stands the command with all its terrible sanctions of thunder and lightnings. If this command is now in force sister S. and all the rest must stand condemned at the dread tribunal of God, for they all break that commandment as much as we who do not pretend to keep it." The speciousness of B.'s reasoning is a great deal more likely to lead saints into bondage, than what he has said of sister Stowe. He begins in the very onset to mislead the mind. He quotes "Let no man go out of his place on the seventh day," and says, there stands the command with all its terrible sanctions of thunder and lightnings, and then says sister S. and Br. Bates and all the rest must stand condemned at the dread tribunal of God, for they all break that *commandment*. Now I say this is not a commandment, but a command given to the children of Israel twenty days before they heard that terrible thunder and lightning at mount Sinai, where the ten commandments was made known to them by the Almighty God's speaking them all out in an audible voice, and then writing them with his own finger on tables of stone. These are all the commandments that God ever gave to man, and they were as equally binding on the stranger, (the Gentile) that was within their gates, as on the Jew. Every one can see how difficult it would be for a man well versed in scripture to remember every direction, or a "thus sayeth the Lord," for a commandment, especially the millions who cannot read. They were of that character, of so few words, that God directed them to "bind them for a sign upon their hands, and they shall be as a frontlet between thine eyes," ("that the Lord's law may be in thy *mouth.*" Exo. xiii: 9,) "and thou shalt write them upon the posts of thy house, and on thy gates." Num. xv: 38-40; Deut. vi: 8, 9. This, God's code of Laws was put into the Ark. Deut. x: 5. And he says that "one law shall be to him that is home born and to the stranger that sojourneth with you." Exo. xii: 49. Now Moses' code of laws was written in a book and placed in the same ark. Deut. xxxi: 24-26. This law from the xiv. ch. and onwards, and in Lev. was to be read to the whole assembly once in seven years; see xxxi: 10-12, and Neh. viii: 1-6. Six hours, reading from morning to noon. But the ten commandments as in Exo. xx: 1-17, can be read in three minutes. If you want to understand God's code of laws separately set forth and enforced, see from iv. to xiv. of Deut. His reasons for giving them to the Jews, vii: 6-8, and x: 22. He tells them they shall not add nor diminish from them. Deut. iv: 2. (Mind this.) "The man for gathering sticks (either to kindle a fire for his comfort, or cook some food, B. says,) was by the command stoned to death."

This is all supposition; nobody knows what he gathered sticks for, or what size they were; he was stoned to death for it, and so we might be now if the law of Moses was in force. Let it be distinctly understood, that God's code of laws, which comprises the ten commandments, does not forbid us to kindle fires on his Sabbath; nor require us to stay in our houses, nor forbid us to assemble together to worship; neither does it forbid us to administer to the sick on his Sabbath, nor do any *work* of absolute necessity. These I propose to treat upon more at large, under the head *Scriptural Observance of the Sabbath.*

Barnabas says, "if the covenant is not altered, amended nor repealed, then it means just what it says. 'Thou shalt not do any work,' stands out in bold relief against those who talk so much about the command, but never yet pretend to keep it. If they say they have a right to alter the phrase," &c. Now we answer, that we never have attempted to alter it. It is perfectly right, and your bare assertion, in the absence of any kind of proof, does not, nor ever will prove, that we do not refrain from work on the Sabbath, according to the commandment, as set forth in the Scriptures.

Two kinds of work are specified or inferred in the law of Moses. "In the sweat of thy face shalt thou eat bread," &c. The way this is done, "man goeth forth to his work and to his labor until evening." This of course includes from the first day to the seventh. Then Sunday is the first working day of the six. This is distinguished *servile* work, because in Lev. xxiii. chap. and xxviii. and xxix. ch. of Numbers, the Lord's Sabbath and the Jewish Sabbaths of holy convocations are all brought to view, so that from the 14th day of the first month to the 22d, is the feast of unleavened bread with offerings, and fifty days from the wafe sheaf or resurrection is another. See Lev. xxiii: 16-18, and then from the first day of the 7th month until the 23d of the same, viz. 1st, 10th, 15th and 23d. The eight last days is a continual feast. Now the Sabbath of the Lord God must inevitably be included in this last eight day feast of Tabernacles; once every year, and very frequently on the first and tenth day Sabbaths, and so from the passover feast to the end of unleavened bread, always must include the weekly Sabbath every year; sometimes on a feast day, which John calls "an high day." Now the order of these Jewish Sabbaths and feasts. God says of them "*every thing upon his day, besides* the Sabbaths of the Lord," &c. All the work was to be performed in these feasts, come on what day they did, besides the offerings on the Sabbath of the Lord. Lev. xxiii: 37, 38. Well, what was the work for every weekly Sabbath? See Num. xxviii: 9, and on Sabbath two lambs, besides the daily, which was two more; see 3d v. So we see here were always four lambs, with the meats, &c. offered every seventh day, and sometimes thirty bullocks, rams and lambs; and in all of the Jewish Sabbaths except that on the tenth of the seventh month, it is expressly said "ye shall do no *servile work* therein." Now all this was work and labor, but it was ceremonial worship and obedience to God, hence it was not *servile* work. It is explained in Exo. xii: 16, "No manner of work shall be done save that which every *soul* must eat. That only may be done." What will you do with all these commands, Barnabas. Did they not have to go out of their places after God gave them the law from mount Sinai? Did they not assemble for worship? Did they not prepare them food to eat, think ye, after the manna ceased? and did not the Saviour say of his disciples, when reproached for eating corn on the Sabbath day by the Pharisees, that they were guiltless? Was it wrong to take it without leave? See Deut. xxiii: 24, 22. Was not the work of circumcision always going on every weekly Sabbath? Now Jesus being the Lord of the Sabbath, shows us under the Gospel, where he transposes these ten commandments from the tables of stone, and gives them in our minds and writes them on our hearts; shows us that this work or labor on the Sabbath, were henceforth acts of necessity and mercy, instead of *servile work* because our mode of worshipping God was entirely changed. Hence Jesus said, "My Father worketh hitherto and I work." John v: 17. See what kind of work, xvii: 4. "Done the will of God, finished his work," after supper. See also iv: 34, and v: 36. See his good works, x: 25, 32. This then was the work that Jesus and his Father were doing, and for these he is called a notorious Sabbath breaker. Well he is now doing a marvellous work. Hab. i: 5, yet ye will not believe. "It is time for the Lord to work for men have made void thy law." Psl. cxix.

It does not follow that men shall be put to death now for violating the Sabbath, any more than for violating the first, fifth, seventh, or all the commandments—for the penalty of death follows the violation of every one of the commandments.

1st commandment: "Thou shalt have no other Gods." See Deut. xiii: 6-10 and Exo. xxii: 20.

2d. "Thou shalt not make any image." Deut. xiii: 12, 16.

3d. "Thou shalt not profane my name." Lev. xxiv: 16, 22, 23.

4th. "Remember the Sabbath day." Num. xv: 32, 33, 36.

5th. "Honor thy father and thy mother." Lev. xx: 9.

6th. "Thou shalt not kill." Lev. xxiv: 21 and 17.

7th. "Thou shalt not commit adultery." Lev. xx: 10.

8th. "Thou shalt not steal." Joshua vii: 20, 21 and 25.

9th. "Thou shalt not witness falsely." Deut. xix: 16, 17, 19, 21.

10th. "Thou shalt not covet." Jos. vii: 20, 25.

All of the commandments together. Num. xv: 30, 31; see also Deut. xxviii: 15-67.

If these were all to be enforced now, there would be but a small remnant of the ten hundred millions now living, left upon the earth. If it is proper to enforce the fourth, it is the whole. How clear that all of these death penalties were annulled with the Jewish dispensation.

When Jesus begins to promulgate his Gospel, the stoning system is all broken up; see his admirable sermon on the mount. Matt v: 38-48. "Ye have heard that it hath been said an eye for an eye and a tooth for a tooth, but I say unto you that ye resist not evil, but whosoever shall smite thee on thy right cheek, turn to him the other also," &c. &c. Here we see that all the followers of Jesus are to be peace men, or non-resistants, an entire change in administering the law. Says Barnabas, this is just what I have been trying to make you believe, that the law, *all* of the *law* that the Jews were subject to in their dispensation was abolished under the Gospel, for we are here under the new testament law, (grace). Not quite so fast: Jesus foreseeing such kind of teaching as this, placed the commandments of God, (on which hung all the law and the prophets,) on an immovable and fixed foundation and carried the teaching and keeping of them clear into the reign of heaven; and any honest man who is seeking for the truth though he be ever so ignorant in other things, will admit, when he reads the 17-19, 21, 27 and 33d verses in this chapter, the force of this truth. What an idea that Jesus should promise such invaluable blessings to his followers after they become immortal only to mislead and tantalize them. This is the tendency of your no commandment no law system. Why Jesus tells you that the teachings of the bible have no other foundations to stand upon. Well the multitude would not believe him then as you and others will not now. See what confusion and shame they suffered and bore in withering silence from his simple direction about enforcing the old law for the violation of the seventh commandment. Here *she* is master, "Now Moses in the law, (not God's code of laws,) commanded that such should be stoned. But what sayest thou?" "Let him that is without sin, cast the first stone at her." The consequence was that the woman was left without an accuser. Thus for once the whole multitude were convinced that the stoning system for violating the commandments was abolished. See John vii: 3-11. Again, you ask, "What type or part of the law was fulfilled by Christ keeping the seventh day, or in our keeping it?" Answer—"Love is the fulfilling of the law." "If ye keep my commandments ye shall abide in my love, even as I keep my Father's commandments and abide in his love." John xv: 10. "This is *my commandment* that ye love one another as I have loved you." 12 verse. Again, Jesus says in Matt. xxii: 37-40, where he includes all of the commandments that love to God and love to our neighbor, is the whole law and the prophets, i. e. that this is the substance of the whole ten commandments. The great one on the first table, the second on the second table of stone. Paul tells the Hebrews that the *law* having a shadow of good things to come cannot make the comers thereunto perfect. This is the *law* of Moses. The ten commandments, the *law* which God audibly gave from his own mouth, is the one that Jesus here refers to, and the only one that he kept abiding in his Father's love. Isaiah says, "He will magnify the law and make it honorable." You know he dishonored the law of Moses by abolishing sacrifices and offerings altogether, and nailing it to his cross. It appears to me that any child, anxious for the truth, would see this distinction. But no, you seem determined on abolishing the whole. You see that Jesus' commandment, John xiii: 34; xv: 12, is the very essence of his Father's and is given exclusively for the church; but his Father's was, and is for the whole human family, and the fourth contains the Sabbath. Now do you see what Jesus means when he says he came not to destroy the law but to fulfill, and don't you understand him to, that this law will stand after the heavens and the earth are passed away. Here then is how and where he fulfilled the law, or as you ask to know, a part of the *law*, for in keeping the commandments he certainly kept the Sabbath; see Mark vi: 2, and Luke iv: 16, 31. This, then, is the way we fulfill the law, by keeping the very same seventh-day Sabbath. There is but two codes of laws brought to view here, viz. God's and Moses'. Don't you see here he has fulfilled the first and abolished the last. You take this rule with you to your favorite texts, viz. Col. ii: 14-17; 2d Cor. iii, and Gal. ii. and v., where you say the commandments, the law of God, and the Sabbath, are abolished; and you will find the same distinction. God never gave Paul, nor you, nor any one else, any more liberty to preach that *his law* was abolished in this, or any other way, than he did to preach that there was no salvation for man. Don't you preach that man should obey the law of God, and when man obeys as Jesus did, don't he fulfill the *law?* Can you tell how man can fulfill it without obeying the *whole* law? You say that will bring us into circumcision. How can that be, when he has, as I have just stated, abolished all the ceremonial part of the law of Abraham and Moses. Again, you say, the only reason given in the bible why the Sabbath was ever kept was, that the Israelites might remember that God brought them out of Egypt. Deut. v: 15. Your objection to the answer that was given by C. Stowe, and reiterating the question, as you have the above answered one, and challenging all who desire to be under the law to prove the contrary, in B. A. Dec. 2d, only goes for proof of your ignorance, or wilfull misunderstanding of God's commandment. If the fourth commandment in Exo. xx: 11, as she quoted and you dissent from it, is not the reason given why we should keep the Sabbath on the seventh day, as directed in the ninth and tenth verses, then it would be impossible to understand the simple word of the Lord. Because God has used the words "command *thee*" to keep the Sabbath, in Deut. v: 15, every other word or form of speech where God requires the keeping of the Sabbath, is made void by you. What is the signification of commands? Is it not to appoint, enjoin, and require by authority? Does it not mean the same as to say "Remember the Sabbath day and keep it holy."—"*Thou shalt not labor or do any work on the Sabbath day.*" Exo. xx: 8-10. Once more, God says, "Ye shall keep the Sabbath." Again, "Wherefore the children of Israel shall keep the Sabbath—for a perpetual covenant. *For* in six days the Lord made heaven and earth, and on the seventh day he rested and was refreshed." xxxi: 14, 16, 17. You see the word command is also used in the 16th verse, for the fifth commandment, and because it is omitted in Exo. xx: 12, according to your rule it is not valid. But it is not so—God speaks as positively and understandingly when he says "*ye shall*," as when he says "I command you." Again, you say—"If Christ did not virtually annul the fourth commandment when he began his public ministry, *then the Jews were* RIGHT IN KILLING HIM AS A NOTORIOUS SABBATH BREAKER. He travelled about and did much work on the Sabbath."

In your second article you offer as proof Luke iv: 18-20. There certainly is no proof of the law's being annulled here. You then quote xvi: 16. "The law and the prophets were until John," &c. This in your whole argument for annulling the fourth commandment. Read the next verse, "And it is easier for heaven and earth to pass, than for one tittle of the law to fail." Now don't a law fail when it passes away? Yes. How then can this law fail till heaven and earth passes? This was virtually showing how impossible it would be for one tittle of the law of God to fail. Here Jesus reverts to the seventh commandment, 18th verse, and shows that the law of the decalogue was what he meant. But he does not say that any law was annulled here. If you say that any part of the law of Moses was abolished here, you upset all the foundation that infidelity raises to overthrow the whole law of God. I wonder that all the second advent editors are not out against you, for if this be true they have no more foundation for their no-law and no-commandments of God system to stand upon than many who are hung on the gallows for venturing to practice after such teaching, by violating the eighth and sixth commandment. I am aware that their Judge Advocate, Joseph Marsh of Rochester, N. Y. has filed in his plea, (see Advent Harbinger, Nov. 9th,) that *we* are under the law of grace, the new testament, and not the law of Moses, which he asserts embraced the ten commandments. Why does not the law of grace save thieves and murderers and liars from the gallows here, and eternal death hereafter. (Rev. xxi: 8.) Answer—because there is no *precept* by which it can be done out of the law of commandments, which was made for *all men*, Jew and Gentile. How would murderers and robbers understand their sentence, viz. You are to be hung until you are dead for violating the law of the new testament, and may the Lord have mercy on you for violating his law of grace. Stop, says the American, you are bound to show me the precept. I ask where it is to be found if the commandments are abolished? Oh, sir, but you have violated the spirit of them. Well, but do tell me, sir, how I have violated the spirit of a law that you say was abolished and forever done away more than eighteen hundred years ago. I am ignorant, I never professed religion, I do not understand the meaning of grace in the new testament—I pray you, sir, don't hang an innocent man.

I have already shown what they tell us that their foundation is for the abolition of God's law; it is in Gal. ii.; Cor. iii, and Col. ii: 14-17. The very day that our Lord was nailed to the cross—(every writer that I remember to have read before on this subject begins at the cross, where Paul directs us to look for the abolition of offerings and oblation, Moses' ceremonial mode of worship)—but you have attempted, without proof, to show that this was done three years before, and that without a shadow of proof that the fourth commandment, or any of them, was done away.

In this second article, you cite us for the same proof to Col. ii: 8-17. How unfortunate for your argument; first that Christ annulled the *law*, and of course the Sabbath, when he began to preach, according to Luke iv: 18-20, and xvi: 16. And then in another place quote Col. ii: 8-17, for the same point of time. How could Christ annul any law twice. First, at his preaching and second at his death, three and a half years apart. Your argument is groundless and futile; therefore the uncalled for blasphemous language of yours, that the Jews were right in killing him (the Son of God) as a notorious Sabbath breaker, will fall on your guilty head. Hear the proof: "They that forsake the law praise the wicked.—He that turneth away his ear from hearing the law, even his *prayer* shall be *abomination.*" See also James ii: 10. Once more, the law that Jesus says shall not pass away, &c. Luke xvi: 17, is proved to be the same as in ch. x: 25-28. Jesus says, how readest thou? what is written in the law? He answers by quoting the two great commandments in the law, in Matt. xxii: 36-40—the same as given in ch. v: 17-19, the keeping of which *then* and *thenceforward* would make them of great esteem in the reign of heaven. Compare also xix: 16-19 with Luke xviii: 18-20. If Jesus' promise of eternal life by our keeping the law of—or, and commandments fails us here, then all his new testament teaching, the "law of grace," so termed, will fail with it.

In conclusion, you call us foolish adventists, and wish to know who has bewitched us? Answer—not the strictly keeping the holy Sabbath and other commandments, but by listening to, or following such unrighteous and deceptive teachings as you set forth. No marvel that you would like to preach it in all the sectarian synagogues in the land, if they would hear you. Fallen Babylon is a more suitable place for such teaching than you will ever find any where else. John describes their condition, Rev. xviii: 2. But I pass. There is but one more remark of yours that I deem worthy of a reply, and I should not most probably have reviewed your articles, only for the defence of God's law and the suffering little flock, my brethren, who are endeavoring to stand where John, in his vision, saw them at this present hour, viz. In their patient waiting time, "keeping the commandments of God and the faith of Jesus."

You say, "If a tree may be known by its fruits, we have a woeful tree here. First, *shut door*; next, *seventh-day Sabbath*, or the bondage of the law; next, Oh, it would be a shame to speak of those things which are done of them in secret. God grant them repentance which is unto life." That we believe in the shut door, and seventh-day Sabbath, is true; that we wash one another's feet, as Jesus taught, and greet one another as Paul has taught, is true of a great portion of those who keep the Sabbath and believe in the past and present truth. If you mean these, that it be a shame to speak of, we answer that we do it openly and avowedly, and teach and practice the same wherever we go, and prove it clearly by the scriptures. If there is any thing secretly practiced by us, it is as much unknown to the church as it is to you. The days of J. Turner and some other leaders of fanaticism in Maine, I trust, have about all subsided, since they have crawled into the Laodocean state of the church. If you know of any thing that we secretly practice in our worship or service of God, that which is a shame to us, we are not unwilling for you to make it as public as you please. We have no faith nor fellowship for any such thing, neither have we any claim on them.

As the editor of the Bible Advocate and yourself are aiming at the one object, viz. the abolition of God's holy Sabbath, and the treading down God's truth seeking children; he is approbating and upholding you in your disguise; we are therefore left to conjecture. From some marks which I have seen under your two coverings, I am very strongly inclined to believe that your real name is Jacob Weston of New Ipswich, N. H. If I am wrong, then what I am about to state will not apply to Barnabas. If I am right in the real character, then I shall discharge *another* duty by exposing an enemy to both God and man, under the cloak of the apostle Barnabas, and beneath that a sheepskin laced round the body of a WOLF, "speaking great words against the most high, thinking to change times and laws." Your unrighteous thrusts, to put down and destroy God's honest children, who are endeavoring to live by every word of God, seems to be in perfect keeping with your wayward, backslidden course. It is you, sir, that have been practising things in secret, which are a shame, and a disgrace, and a stigma upon the cause which you profess. Now lay off that apostolic cloak which you have taken to cover your deformed and deceptive arts. The reason why you have assumed this garb to oppose your opponent, C. Stowe, is to *some* very obvious. You knew that she was acquainted with some of your ungodly proceedings. You had not forgotten the false promises and pretences which you had resorted to, first, to obtain her money, and then to keep her out of it. After repeated calls for it, you at length sent it to her, stating that the reason why you did not answer her letters, was, because you had not the money, and you did not write her, *because it would subject her to pay the postage*, as *you could not*! and then in an insulting manner to dictate a letter, teaching her how she should write to you.

After this squall had blown over and things had become more settled, a mysterious letter is presented to sister Stowe, signed Lydia B. Weston, setting forth your helpless condition—not actually asking for money, because it would not comport with her severe remark about *"dying first,"*—but to draw still more on her sympathy, it states that her husband had fell and lamed, or sprained his ancle, &c. &c. Sister S., although about forty miles from this scene of suffering and distress, requested a friend and neighbor of yours to ascertain what was needed, and she was ready to assist, notwithstanding all the past. Your house was visited and inquiry made for the lame man, but he was away. "Well, you have heard from Washington?" Your wife. L. B. Weston, replied, "she did not know how?" [Another statement is, "have you heard from Washington?" "No." "Have you not written to Washington?" (or sister Stowe.) "No."] The messenger was much surprised! "Well, are you in need of any thing?." "No, we have all that we need at present!" and she then proceeded to enumerate all the comfortable things she had.

From this it is evident that your wife was an entire stranger to this letter and its contents. Who wrote this forged letter? The capitals, it was said by those who examined it, were J. Weston's, but the hand-writing was rather finer than his. When you have been told of this your reply has been that sister Stowe *lies* if she says that I wrote that letter! It is all in vain for you to reiterate such assertions. The question is, where is the person in New Ipswich, whose hand-writing will compare with this letter, and who is so interested in your behalf that they will even contradict your wife, who manages your household affairs; and state falsehoods, and then commit the high crime of FORGERY, by affixing her name to their assertions, to obtain for you what you did not need; and among other things, what could they mean by lying so about your lame leg? If you can find this *daring*, loving, and insultingly magnanimous person in your neighborhood, do, for the sake of the community at large, expose him, and let this sister and others whom you have maligned, have their real name. And then if you go to Nelson again, to preach the doctrine of the second advent by a notice in the Bible Advocate of July 30th, or Aug. 5th, "Squire Hale will not refuse you the use of the meeting house, because of said *forgery*." And possibly they may then sympathise with you more in respect to your poverty in having but one feather bed in your house, &c. &c., when it is well known that you have three, and other things in proportion.

That must have been rather a stirring exhortation that you gave the man who called to see you, a short time since; that the Lord was coming in about three weeks. Did you cite him to the Bible Advocate of Dec. 9, and tell him to read the caption that your old friend Timothy Cole had published for you; that the *time for the Lord's coming was revealed*, and that you felt so impressed with the truth of the above that you could not hold your peace any longer, &c. Well, possibly he did feel the force of the truth, that the Lord would soon come, but it soon vanished from him when you read the note for twenty dollars, in his favor, which he now presented, and which you told him was not negotiable, and that there was no law by which he could collect it. Did you not feel rather singular, for a professed ambassador of Christ, to be told by this man "how strange it appeared to him that *you* should go and put such a note on to an old woman." [This is an old lady, partially deranged, who having a little money, finally consented to loan it to him on a note for interest.] It seems you had consulted a lawyer, to know whether it could be collected in her life time for her.

Are you aware of the heinousness of these things? Did you ever read the life of the pious Dr. Dod of England, who was hung for *forgery*; people no doubt liked his preaching. I know a professed minister, who, not many years since, was elected pastor of a church, with but two or three dissenting votes, in a place situated in North latitude 41° 33', and longitude 70° 53' W., who was told by one of his members, in a church meeting, that he had committed the high crime of *forgery*, which he did not attempt to deny. The member for daring to utter this and connected things, was suspended from their communion until he should make ample satisfaction. The minister was retained, and a great revival, by his exertions, immediately followed, and numbers were added to *their* church. So, you see, ministers are not to be known by their great preaching and revivals. "Ye shall know them by their fruits." So, I trust, the second advent believers will know you hereafter. They will also know that God never employed a righteous man to stigmatize and attempt to make void his Sabbath and commandments. That is, and ever has been, the work of "the Devil and his angels." "Surely the Lord God will do nothing but he reveals his secrets unto his servants, the prophets." Amos. But "he that turneth away his ear from hearing the *law*, even his prayer shall be abomination." All men are liable to err and make mistakes, but when persevered in, under disguise, they are to be rebuked.

# To The Editor Of The "Advent Harbinger."

SIR:—After your repeated and unsuccessful attempts to stigmatize, put down, demolish, and forever abolish the TEN WORDS, the law and commandments of the living God, the only foundation for the bible, you come forth in the A. H. of Nov. 9th, and say "We are not under the law (of Moses,) but under (the law of) grace, the *New Testament*, and now all we want to know is, does the NEW TESTAMENT *either by precept or example* require us *to keep* ANY day as a SABBATH?... We do not want your inferences, but plain, direct NEW TESTAMENT testimony; nothing else will do in a case of this character and importance." Your term, law of Moses, according to *all* your teachings on this subject, includes the law of commandments. We have given it to you in our work on the Sabbath, and again in the Way Marks, pp. 76-78. Why do you still continue to demand proof, until you have found out some new method to explain those texts away. It is evident that your object on this point is to confuse the minds of your readers and not give them the clear word of God. What would Christ and his apostles have done for proof from the old testament, if your new restricted rule had been laid before them? and you had told them seven months previous, (April 28th,) that the law of commandments, when they were abolished, were incorporated into the new testament, or *law of Christ*. And now we are under the *law of grace*. It appears to me that Jesus would have replied as he did on one occasion, "Get thee behind me Satan." Is the law of Christ and the law of grace, synonymous terms? or are you so privileged now in the high station which you have assumed, that you can change the name of *your* NEW LAW once in seven months, and make Christ and grace the same. It is impossible for any man to depart from the clear word and abide in the truth. Call the commandments of God what you will, and incorporate them where you will, you are bound, as I have told you before, to show the precept, (i. e. how they read,) and then if you refer us to the teachings of Jesus and his apostles, and the Revelation of John, you will only point us directly to the ten commandments of God, which as clearly proves that they are not, nor ever have been abolished, any more than the prophecies of Isaiah, Jeremiah or Ezekiel; and just so sure as Jesus has spoken the truth, that eternal life is obtained by the keeping of them, and that James wrote by inspiration, we are to be judged by them; and not by what you have misnamed them, the *law of grace*. How can the commandments of God be abolished, and yet the keeping of them give us an entrance into the city. Rev. xxii: 14. And yet if they are abolished, as you assert, who can ever know when they fail in one precept or when they keep the whole? Your attempt to incorporate God's law, after—as you say—it has been abolished, and now enforce it without a precept, because it is all incorporated in the new testament, is a thousand times more inconsistent than a temporal millenium. "Grace is the gift of God." Then, according to your logic, this is the law that we are now under. How shall we enumerate all the gifts of God, and incorporate them into the new testament? One thing I know, you will never mend the law of God: It is as immutable as the sun in the heavens! and it would be far easier work for you and all of like faith to blot out that luminary than to prove that one jot or tittle of the ten commandments had failed by being changed or abolished. I intend to prove this from the new testament as I pass on, and if you and your adherents will still misrepresent the plain teaching and lead others to do so, then the words of Jesus will surely condemn you, and you "will be in no esteem in the reign of heaven."

First Pillar For No Sabbath.

There are four Pillars in the temple of your no-Sabbath, no-commandment system, which we are always referred to as positive proof that you are right. Now if I can prove from the new testament that they and all others that you may present, are only your "*inferences*," (and you say you don't want any,) what will you do? Further—these pillars of yours, be it *forever remembered and never forgotten*, are fixed at the day of the crucifixion of our Lord. Say, if you like, it was in A.D. 33. This is the point where you have to bring your scripture to prove any thing of the kind, i. e., if you go one week on either side of the death of our blessed Lord, your arguments or pillars, all fall to the ground. Now, by this plain rule, we will try the first two no-Sabbath texts: First—1 Rom. xiv: "One man esteemeth one day above another, another esteemeth every day *alike*; let every man be fully persuaded in his own mind. He that regardeth the day, regardeth it unto the Lord." Read the whole chapter; Paul's whole argument here is against their feasts, and this of course included their feast days, which some esteemed and others did not. "Destroy not him with thy *meat* for whom Christ died," says Paul, 15th verse. Compare this with the first, third, and last four verses, where he closes with "He that doubteth is damned if he eat, because he eateth not of faith," 23d verse, and then tell me if you can, what other day or days is here brought to view than feast days, as in Lev. xxiii chapter, which Hosea said were to cease. This same chapter, 3d and 38th verses, positively designates and separates the Sabbath of the Lord God from all these feast Sabbaths, or days; also Num. xxviii: 9. Now as God's Sabbath was not a feast Sabbath, it was impossible to connect it with these. And that is not all—it is not even alluded to here—only guessed at from among the feast days. Once set such a rule as this at work and there is not a law in christendom that would restrain men. For all will have one day for a holy, or holiday in the week. Now give them, by your bible rule, their choice, and I don't believe that Satan himself would bring them to order. Oh, but we have a law that the first-day shall be regarded as the Sabbath. Well, that is what you now contend for, and so does almost all christendom, and still it is an unrighteous and an unscriptural law, because the first day is not, nor never was, the Sabbath. You have no right by this rule to fix on any day, and yet every body would be right if every day was kept. But, you may say, it means we shall have no day for the Sabbath. It does not read so. It says, "let every man be persuaded in his own mind," and if that were the case, what kind of order would there be in God's house. I ask if there be a rational being on earth that for a moment would believe that God ever intended to give the whole human family such a choice as this, after he had required them to keep the Sabbath day. No, he is a God of order, and he sanctified and set apart the seventh day for man and beast. Does not the beast require rest now as much as he did 1900 years ago? Who is to advocate for them, if man does not? The great mass of professed christians are insisting on the first day for one of these days, and it is not at all likely that they would ever refer to this test for this purpose were it not to destroy the idea of a seventh-day Sabbath. See work on the Sabbath, pp. 11-12. This subject is continued from the xiiith chapter, where the apostle had been enforcing the commandments, and one is equally binding as the other, except the fourth, which is more insisted upon than the rest. This letter is dated Corinthus, A.D. 60.

Second Pillar For No Sabbath.

Col. ii: 14-17.—"Blotting out the hand writing of ordinances that was against us; which was contrary to us, taking it out of the way; nailing it to his cross." Now Paul says it was the hand-writing of ordinances that was blotted out. You say it was the Sabbath, because he further says, "Let no man therefore judge you in meat, or in drink, or in respect of an holy day, or of the new moon, or of the Sabbath days, which are a shadow of things to come," &c. Now I say that the Sabbath of the Lord God is not included in this text. 1st. Because it never did belong to the hand-writing of ordinances. 2d. It never is called an ordinance in the scriptures; it is a commandment. 3d. God's Sabbath never was taken out of our way because it was against us. Jesus says it was made for us, (for man.) Then pray tell me, if you can, why Jesus has taken away from us the very thing, (the Sabbath) he had said was made for us? You see this is impossible; but he did take away at the very hour that he yielded up his life, the ceremonial worship of sacrifice and oblation, because *his* blood was now shed once for all for the whole world, therefore the shedding of bullocks blood, here at this hour, ceased forever; see also Heb. x: 1-10, particularly the 9th verse. The angel Gabriel's testimony is directly to this point; Dan. ix: 27. Therefore the mode of worshipping God, in the law of Moses, ceased forever. But all of this no more affected God's code of laws, the ten commandments, than the shining of the sun would upon the inhabitants of Massachusetts after he had gone down below the western horizon. The "hand-writing of ordinances" is what Moses wrote with his hand in a book and put it into the ark with the tables of stone: which tables were not the hand-writing of either God, or man, but written by the finger of God. Deut. xxxi: 25-26. Neither can it ever be proved that God's law on these tables of stone, was a shadow—it is a substance. Paul says the things that were nailed to the cross here, were shadows; see 17th verse. Now if the Lord's Sabbath, the fourth commandment, was taken out here, and forever erased from the tables of stone—*where is the evidence?* Further, if it was a shadow, as you say, would not all the other nine commandments be shadows too? See if you can make the first and second ones, shadows; if you can, the worship of idols is just as valid as the worship of God; and so of the third—where would be the penalty of taking God's name in vain, or to steal, or murder, or commit adultery? You see the idea itself is ridiculous. I know you say the spirit of them is as binding as ever. I ask how are we to know what the spirit of any thing is, without the precept (the letter) to guide us? It is impossible for any human being to know that it is wrong to worship idols and bow down to them unless it read so in the scriptures. If the apostle has taught it so, he has quoted from the decalogue. Thus you see the commandments can no more be abolished than salvation. In the 20-22d verses, Paul further explains, and says, "Why are ye subject to ordinances which are to perish?" Why perish? because "they are after the doctrines and commandments of men." "Touch not, taste not, handle not." Now, if these are not the ordinance of the ceremonial law, the hand-writing of Moses, they are nothing; see also Eph. ii: 15, and Heb. vii: 16. The holy day, new moon and Sabbath days were their holy convocation, which, with the new moon and Sabbaths is the same that is connected with their feasts, as in Rom. xiv, and as distinctly separate, as I have shown in Lev. xxiii: 3, 38, and Num. xxviii: 9. Now I say God's law containing the Sabbath is not even mentioned here. Their Sabbath days, and not God's Sabbath days is here abolished; as Hosea said they should be, ii: 11. It would be far more reasonable to assert that Paul had abolished all the ordinances in 20-22 verses. But who undertakes to say that baptism and the Lord's Supper are abolished here. Nobody. Why? Because neither of them are the hand-writing of ordinances, but they are equally as much so, and as certainly made for us as the Sabbath is. Jesus says it was made for man. You say it was made for the Jews only. Shall the scriptures decide this, "MAN that is born of a woman is of few days and full of trouble." "MAN dieth and wasteth away; yea, MAN giveth up the ghost and where is he—So MAN lieth down and riseth not till the heavens be no more."—Job. "And as it is appointed unto MAN once to die, but after this the judgment."—Paul. Now just as certain as the Jews and Gentiles are the "man" alluded to here, just in the same sense and no other, is he alluded to by Jesus in Mark ii: 27—"The Sabbath was made for MAN,"—Jew and Gentile, for every living human being. Therefore it is impossible, yea it is a contradiction of terms to say that the Sabbath of the Lord God, which was made for man, just as much as the day of judgment is to judge him, was taken out of his way, because it was *contrary* to him, and against him, or that the Sabbath is an ordinance or a shadow, but all the seven Jewish convocation Sabbaths that were nailed to the cross, were shadows, as in Heb. x: 1-10. The woman was also made for man, in the same sense. See how your rule will work here. This letter is from Rome, A. D. 64.

Third Pillar For No-Sabbath, No-Commandments.

Gal. ii.-vi. chapters. Here we are told that the whole law and commandments are abolished. I say the man was never yet born that can prove it. You say *"we want none of your inferences."* Neither do we want yours, unless you can back them up by scripture testimony. Paul begins with the Gospel; in his second chapter he brings up the law of circumcision, and goes on to show that it is abolished. Just look at the 7th and 8th verses, where he begins his argument, and then 11-14th. His controversy with Peter respecting this point and eating, meets; then the 16th, 18th and 21st verses show again most clearly that he is contrasting the Gospel of Christ with this law of meats and circumcision. He now passes through the 3d chapter, (so much relied on for the abolition of all *law*,) without intimating any other law whatever. In the 4th chapter, 4th verse, he says, God sent forth his son, made, or born under the law. What law? Answer—the law of Moses. There is not an intimation of the law of commandments here; neither is there an intimation in God's law, relating to Jesus, but there is in Moses'. In the 10th verse he begins again, and says "yea, observe days and months and times and years." These are the same feast days that I have been treating of in the two first Pillars, viz. Rom. xiv. and Col. ii., for when he comes to the 21st verse, he says again, "tell me ye that desire to be under the *law*, do ye not hear the law." What is it? Why, Abraham had two sons, one by his bond maid, Hagar, the other by Sarah, his wife. These two women represent the two covenants. Hagar represents mount Sinai, where God gave the first covenant. Hagar also answers to the present Jerusalem, now in bondage; Sarah represents the second covenant, (which gives entrance into the) *New* Jerusalem. See 9.

In the fifth chapter he begins again with circumcision, 2d and 3d verses. In the 4th verse he says, "Whosoever of you are justified by the *law* are fallen from grace." This is the law of circumcision; see 6th and 11th verses: "If I yet preach circumcision, why do I yet suffer persecution." Now see the contrast at the close of his argument. Here is the law of God; see 14th verse: "For *all* the law is fulfilled in one word, even this, thou shalt love thy neighbor as thyself." This was his very expression to the Romans, four years previous; see xiii: 9. Here he has cited them to the second table of stone in God's law, in respect to their neighbor, which is alone, the clear meaning; and we are saved by "keeping the commandments of God and faith of Jesus."—Rev. xii: 12; xxii: 14. Paul did not stop to explain about these two covenants, but merely alluded to them to show the two entirely different modes of worship under the two dispensations. His letter to the Hebrews six years afterwards, explains, "Now the first covenant had *ceremonies* of *divine* service and a worldly sanctuary," ix: 1. Now the covenant ITSELF was in the ark; see 4th verse. Now these rites and ceremonies which stood in meats and drinks, &c. were carnal ordinances, a figure for the time then present, until the reformation, or coming of the new covenant. Not a syllable about the fourth commandment in 4th verse being a figure, or ordinance or ceremony, or being done away. Why? Because in the preceding chapter, 6-10th verses, he shows is the new or second covenant, which was to succeed the first, and Jesus was to be the mediator of it. Now the first covenant was the ten commandments, with ceremonies, &c. The second covenant is (*my laws*) the same ten commandments, (not as before, on tables of stone,) but in our minds and on our hearts; 10th verse. Connected with this is the testimony of Jesus Christ—proof, Rev. xii: 17; xix: 10, and xiv: 12. This is the New, or Gospel Covenant, which Jesus Christ came to confirm. Then all that was nailed to the cross was the ceremonial law, the Jewish mode of worshipping God. The first covenant the law of God, is here transcribed from the tables of stone and placed on our hearts; see Rom. ii: 15: Heb. viii: 10. This entirely changes the mode of worship, and shows us "without faith it is impossible to please God." If the law of God is not the same in both covenants, with Jew and Gentile, tell me if you can the chapter and verse for the second, or new law of God. It is the very same that Jesus had given in Matt. xxii: 39; the last six commandments. Here he closes this chapter by contrasting the works of the flesh with the fruits of the spirit, and then in the 6th chapter, 12th, 13th and 15th verses, he alludes again to circumcision, and says, in 15th verse, "For in Christ Jesus neither circumcision availeth any thing nor uncircumcision," &c., showing conclusively that the great burthen of his argument from first to last, was to abolish circumcision and vindicate God's law, instead, as you and your adherents will have it, abolish the commandments in the law. I say then in the 5th chapter, 14th verse, he has positively taught us that the law of God was untouched in his argument. Suppose we take his letter to the Romans, to explain how he sustains this law. "If there be any other commandment it is briefly comprehended in this saying, namely, thou shalt love thy neighbor as thyself." xiii: 9. "Therefore love is the fulfilling of the law." In the first place he is here showing us our duty to our neighbor, (not to God), 8-10 verses—for he has quoted only five of the commandments from the second table of stone. Will you say that because he omitted the fifth one, it is abolished;  see his letter to the Ephesians, four years after this: "Honor thy father and thy mother, which is the first commandment, with promise," vi: 2. Now Paul has here quoted from the tables of stone, and this is proof positive that these six are not abolished. But because he has not quoted the first four, will you say *they* are abolished? If you say they are, then you make void the Saviour's words in Matt. xxii: 37, 38; and also Paul's in the 7th chapter, 12th verse, where he says "the law is holy and the commandments holy, just and good." Again, because Jesus, in Matt. v: 19, 21, 27, 33, only quoted the 3d, 6th and 7th commandments, are the other seven abolished? If so, how strange that he should add three more, respecting love to our neighbor, in chapter xix: 18, 19, viz. the 5th, 8th and 9th. And in the 15th chapter quote only one. Further, because he never mentioned the fourth commandment separately, you would have us believe there is none—he abolished it. Then, by the same rule he abolished the first, second, and tenth, for he has not mentioned them. In this case Paul has taught heresy, for he has mentioned the tenth commandment twice in Romans. Paul nowhere speaks of the first four commandments, but he quotes the other six. James only quotes two, the sixth and seventh, for his *perfect royal law of liberty,* by which man is to be judged; but that we might not misunderstand that he meant what he said, that it was a *perfect law,* including the whole ten, he declares that "if we fail with respect to one precept, we become guilty of all." Here you, and all of like faith, must see the fallacy of your reasoning, which is, that because the fourth commandment has not been distinctly expressed, then there is no Sabbath. I say, by your rule, it is just as clear that Jesus and Paul never taught us that we should not worship images, and bow down to idols, for they have never quoted us the precept. But they both have taught us the whole law and commandments; see Matt. xxii: 36-40; Luke x: 25-28; Rom. vii: 12; 1st Cor. vii: 19. The reason, no doubt, why Jesus never quoted the 1st, 2d, 3d and 4th commandments separately was because he never had occasion to use them for an argument with his hearers. Now this certainly explains Paul's meaning in Gal. v: 14, "For all the law is fulfilled in one word, even in this, thou shalt love thy neighbor as thyself." That is—this is the law respecting our duty to one another, as Jesus has taught us in Matt. xxii. This, then, is the *law* from the decalogue. Paul says this law is fulfilled by keeping it, while that which was added to the law (or covenant) is abolished; see Heb. ix. Then here the law of God is established, and not, as you say, abolished. This letter is dated at Rome, A.D. 58.

Fourth And Last Pillar For No-Sabbath, No-Commandments.

2d Cor. iii. Here a host of second advent believers join in with you, and labor to prove that Paul has certainly and positively abolished the commandments of God. Yes, one of your old correspondents, G. Needham, of Albany, has publicly declared to the world that God told him so. Now if I prove him to have uttered a positive falsehood, I suppose he will still be considered in good standing, as a second advent lecturer and coadjutor in carrying forward this work of heresy. If God ever told him any thing about this text, he did not contradict Paul, who spake by the Holy Ghost. The principal verses to sustain this heresy, are 7, 8, 11, 13, 14th, "But if the ministration of death, written and engraven in stones, was glorious, so that the children of Israel could not steadfastly behold the face of Moses for the glory of his countenance, which glory was to be done away, how shall not the ministration of the spirit be rather glorious?... For if that which is done away is glorious, much more that which remaineth is glorious.... And as Moses which put a veil over his face, that the children of Israel could not steadfastly look to the end of that which is abolished. But their minds were blinded, for until this day remaineth the same veil, untaken away in the reading of the old testament, which veil is done away in Christ." Now every bible student must admit that Paul was contrasting the ministration of the Jewish nation with that of his own, the Gospel ministration, (11th v.) under the two dispensations. If Moses' ministry was glorious, then is the Gospel much more so. Now that which was to be done away was not the *decalogue itself*, the ten commandments, but the ministration of it, which was emblematically illustrated by the glory of Moses' countenance, which was only for the time being. This clause refers expressly to the glory of his countenance, and not to the glory of the law on the tables of stone. So also the clause, "that which is abolished," does not refer to the decalogue, but to the ministration of Moses, including what he writes to the Heb. ix: 9-11, and x: 1-10; see particularly 9th verse: "He taketh away the first that he may establish the second." How? Answer—"I will put my law (the same law of the ten commandments) in their inward parts, and write it in their hearts." viii: 10, 5-9. Again, "we are not without law to God, but under the law to Christ." This certainly is the same law and so is the following, "Do we make void the law through faith? God forbid ye, we *establish* the law." It is impossible for this to be the law of ceremonies in Moses' ministration, for that was nailed to the cross, certainly twenty-five years before. Here then it is plain, as in Heb. ix: 4, that the tables of stone, on which was the whole law of God, remained unmoved, to be written on our hearts. No other law of God can be found for this purpose. The 14th verse says, "which veil was done away in Christ." Again, if the commandments were done away here, how could those "who teach them be of great esteem in the reign of heaven;" and how could they teach them without knowing the words from the decalogue? "The law of grace and the law of Christ" would darken counsel without knowledge. If the tables of stone were done away here, where are the commandments referred to so many times in the new testament for us to keep, and how useless for Christ to come at the first advent and write them in our hearts, if they were not to be kept. Now this epistle is dated at Phillippi, A.D. 60; twenty-seven years after the crucifixion.

The date of the other three Pillars, as stated, are, 1st, Rom. xiv: 5, 6, Corinthus, A.D. 60. 2d, Col. ii: 14-17, Rome, A.D. 64. 3d, Gal. ii-vi., Rome, A.D. 58. Now remember what I stated before, that if the commandments or Sabbath ever were abolished, the proof is contained in these four principal texts or Pillars, and it was all done at the crucifixion or death of Jesus; see Col. ii: 11, "nailing it to the cross," (in A.D. 33). Now Paul's first letter to the Corinthians was dated at the same place one year before his second letter, A.D. 59. Here he says, chapter vii: 19, "circumcision is nothing and uncircumcision  is nothing but the *keeping* of the *commandments* of God." Again, we will now go to the chapter to which you exultingly point your readers, for the abolition of this same law and commandments, viz. Rom. vii: 6, "But now we are delivered from the law," &c. What law? Answer—the very same that you have had to make your four Pillars of, viz. the law of Moses, the Jewish ritual. "What shall we say then, is the law sin?" [You say it is.] Paul says, "God forbid," and he quotes the tenth commandment to prove it; 7th verse, and then in the 12th directs us to the whole law of God, thus— "WHEREFORE THE LAW IS HOLY, AND THE COMMANDMENTS HOLY, JUST AND GOOD." Now, I say, here is testimony that all the opposers of God's law cannot impeach, and it utterly demolishes and overthrows every idea that has been presented for the last fifteen hundred years against the whole ten commandments and law of God. It *nails* the *point down twenty-seven years* after the Jewish rites and ceremonials in the law of Moses were nailed to the cross, as you and all of your faith say it was, and fully and clearly sustains all the scriptural arguments herein presented, as in Rom. iii: 31; xiii: 8-10, same year, and Gal. v: 14, two years before, and Eph. vi: 2, six years after. You may object to these dates. If they could be altered and carried back twenty years, it would not help your case, for *without any date*, a child might know that Paul was not even converted to Christianity until years after the ceremonial law was nailed to the cross.

You may contradict Paul if you will, and call out all your *professed* second advent adherents and brethren, (whom you say will not see much of any difference on this subject after they have examined the *new testament,*) and they will not in the least strengthen your arguments unless G. Needham should come *out* again and publicly declare that God also told him that Paul's testimony respecting his law and commandments, was not to be credited. And this he can as readily establish as he can his first blasphemous assertion.

You might still go on and contradict James' *perfect, royal law of liberty*, whose testimony is to the same point and in the same year, and tell John the beloved disciple also, whose testimony is thirty years beyond James', that he ought to have called his *old* commandment, which he received from the FATHER, "which ye have heard from the *beginning*," (1st John ii: 7, and 2d epistle, 4-6 verses.) "*The law of grace*." because that would eventually be the right name that you should give them in 1847, after you had been designated *one* of the two great reformers in the world, to give light on the second coming of Christ, and so make him and James, who had heard their Lord declare that he had kept his Father's commandments; and Luke and Matthew testifying to his declaration that "the law and the prophets hung upon them," and that the teaching and keeping of them would ensure "*great esteem*," and "*eternal life in the reign of heaven*," he would most likely have cited you to the epistle again, and said, read your *sentence*: "He that saith I know him and keepeth not his commandment is a LIAR *and the* TRUTH *is not* IN HIM."

I should not be at all surprised if you called all this *inferential*, irrelevant *New Testament* testimony, because your grand object is to destroy the seventh-day Sabbath. If the Sabbath is not to be found in the commandments of God, then where is it to be found?

If those to whom I dedicate this work believe that I have proved beyond controversy that the commandments are valid and still to be kept, as the Revelation also teaches, xii: 17; xiv: 12; xxii: 14; then they are a *perfect law*, and cannot fail in one point without risking our salvation. Then the seventh-day Sabbath is included or the testimony of Jesus and his Apostle would be false. Again, there is but one Sabbath that was ever required to be kept, in the bible, and that is

*THE* SABBATH.

Jesus kept *the* Sabbath, and when he was giving them the signs of his coming and the end of the world, he pointed them at least thirty-five years after his death, to the very same Sabbath. On the 29th of June last, you replied to J. Gifford's inquiries on this point, and perverted the word, and called THE, *their Sabbath*. You also say, "The day before the resurrection was the Jewish Sabbath, which Christ *kept* in the tomb. When that Sabbath ended, the law of types ended, and of course the *typical* Sabbath ceased—a new dispensation commenced on the first day, which should be observed in commemoration of the death of Christ, until he come." Now look at your *zig-zag* course. First, that the whole law with the decalogue was nailed to the cross. But here, to get rid of this brother's argument, about the Sabbath being kept the day before the resurrection, and after the crucifixion, you stretch out the Sabbath in the fourth commandment about twenty-seven hours, (as long as you wanted it,) and then put it back with the other nine that died the day before.

Here too, you say, "ended the law types, and of course the typical Sabbath," and then about twelve hours after a new dispensation commenced. Your argument looks like this—the Jewish dispensation ended at the preaching of Christ. Oh no, it was at his death—where the law of Moses, with the commandments of God, were *all* nailed to the cross. But stop again—the Sabbath did not end, nor the types, until twenty-seven hours after; and finally—come to think of it—the dispensation did not end until about twelve hours after that, when Christ arose. Surely J. Turner, with all his mesmeric influence, could not do much better. How much better to follow Paul in Col. ii: 14, "blotting out the hand-writing of ordinances (the ceremonial law) and nailing it to the cross" on Friday, the 14th day of the first month, "FINISHED" at 3 o'clock, P. M.—John xix: 30; Mark xv: 33, 37. Again, you say "the Jews were so tenacious about the strict observance of *their* Sabbath, that they would have prevented the disciples fleeing on that day, had they made an attempt to do so; hence for their own salvation, Christ taught his disciples to pray that their flight might not be on that day, not because it would be wrong to *save their lives* on that day, which the Sabbatarian view seems to teach." In the first place Christ never intimated a word about *their* Sabbath; it was THE Sabbath, the same that he had kept. Your sophistical argument about their flight, &c. &c. touches not the main point. Christ did here recognize THE Sabbath of the Lord thirty-five years beyond the time which you say it was abolished. At that time, if it never did before, as you have it, it belonged as much to the Gentile as the Jew, unless you make another attempt to stretch out the Jewish dispensation thirty-five years to cover it. His disciples certainly kept the Sabbath, the day after his death, and you cannot prove by the scriptures that the disciples ever held a meeting but once of an evening on the first day. Therefore you must be very much pushed for a Sabbath, to continually call that day one, as you do, at the same time reiterating, "*we want none of your inferences!*" Luke also recognizes THE Sabbath twenty years beyond the resurrection, and shows that Paul kept it, and the Gentiles also.—Acts xiii: 42, 44. You attempt to destroy all this proof too, because you say this was the Jews' day for worship, and Paul could get a better hearing. Don't you see that the Gentiles invited him to preach to them—they kept the same day, 44th verse. See xvi: 13; here they are by the river's side. Paul's manner was to reason with them on the Sabbath; see xvii: 2, and xviii: 4, 11. So was it the custom of the Saviour; Mark vi: 2, and Luke iv: 16, 31. Now if all this is not *New Testament* evidence enough for *honest* believers, in the absence of any other testimony for an abolition, or change of the Sabbath, then it is because men would rather pervert the word of God than keep it.

God's Code of Laws in the New Testament.

"Why do ye transgress the commandments of God."—Matthew xv: 3.

"What is written in the law, how readest thou?"—Luke x: 26.

"Even as I have kept my Father's commandments."—John xv: 10.

"Yea, we establish the law."—Rom. iii: 31.

"The law is holy and the commandment is holy."—Rom. vii: 12.

"Not subject to the law of God."—Rom. viii: 7, also xiii: 8-10.

"But the commandments of God."—1st Cor. vii: 19; 1st Tim. i: 8.

"For whoever shall keep the whole law," &c.—James ii: 10.


Moses' Code of Laws, by Jesus and His Apostles.

"That is written in *their* law, they hated," &c.—John xv: 25.

"Justified by the law of Moses."—Acts xiii: 39.


"It is written in *your* law, I said, ye are gods?"—John x: 34.

"Have ye not read in the book of Moses."—Mark xii: 26.

"Judged according to *our* law."—Acts xxiv: 6.

"Out of the law of Moses."—xxvii: 23, and xxi: 20, 22, 24, 28.

"And *your* law."—Acts xviii: 15. Paul.

This and much more could be given to show the clear distinction that Jesus and his Apostles and the Jews always kept up between the law of God and the law of Moses. This is why so much confusion pervades our minds, when we read Paul to the Cor., Rom., Gal., and Col. If we carefully read his letter to the Hebrews, his Jewish brethren, we shall see a clearer distinction. In the 7th chapter, and first part of the 8th, he describes the priesthood; the change to Christ in his sanctuary in the heavens, and then the second covenant, the law of God written on our hearts. 9th chapter explains the first covenant, with its appendages, and the change. 10th chapter shows that these appendages never could make us perfect. 9th verse speaks of the change; 16th verse of the law of God again, and the 28th of the law of Moses. These four chapters will give more light respecting the two codes of laws; how one is abolished, except the types, and the other established, than all that ever I read from the pens of these no-commandment professors. May God help us to see the clear light.

# To the Editor of The Bible Advocate.

SIR—I was very glad when learned that your columns were to be opened for the discussion of the Sabbath question, for I thought if you would allow this subject to be fairly brought out, God's holy law would be vindicated and more strictly revered; but I soon see this was, and would be, an unequal warfare. To prevent any one's writing but C. Stowe of N. H., you say her argument will cover, or about cover, the whole ground in favor of the Jewish, or seventh-day Sabbath, and then no one else, until some one had replied against it, &c. This was very well, but I soon perceived that you did not keep the ship on her course. The first part of C. Stowe's article, to cover the whole ground, has never yet appeared, and should it come forth at this late hour of the discussion, it would probably avail as much as you mean it shall in its isolated state. But to prevent what you did publish for her, in the same paper, (Sept. 2d,) you gave your own unscriptural view, to go with it. This, of course, still more prejudiced your hearers, as you had before that stated objections. I am not sorry, however, that it is still going on in some shape, if it is partly in disguise. We hear that you have now on hand five times as much matter against the Sabbath as you have for it. This is all natural enough, God's word has ever been advocated by the minority. And when such blasphemous language against the Saviour we are looking for, was permitted to blacken your columns, and again reiterated that he was right, and you not only let it pass unnoticed, but was endeavoring to screen him by withdrawing his real name from God's children. The inference is, and must be, strong against you. Look at your position now! THE BIBLE ADVOCATE!! Show if you can the chapter and verse where the BIBLE allows any man to advocate God's word, that ever withheld his real name and where those that stood in high places were trying to screen them, because as we should have a good right to suppose, that they were in fellowship with their doctrine. How do the columns of THE BIBLE ADVOCATE look now, since you have opened the way for them to follow your unrighteous course, to debase and still hold up God's holy law as a Jewish ritual, that had been abolished. It looks to me like the same horn that is to "prevail against the saints until the ancient of days comes." "He thought to change times and laws;" (God's laws without doubt.) He, then, through this agency, has been blackening your columns with his iron hoof. The Devil has been too long engaged in this war to pass any one's enclosure, who has left his gate open, without walking in and taking possession. How could you be so careless or wilful, after warring with him as you have done in the past, to leave the way open for him to tread you down. Another thing: In your paper of Dec. 23d, you say, "Br. Turner, have you sent your second article on the Sabbath? We have not received it." Why in so much haste for this wonderful promised article, to overthrow history, after he has overthrown himself by the bible? Why not publish some of the so much manuscript you have already on hand? I cannot help thinking, after all, that you have no faith in your own argument of a no-Sabbath, no-commandment system, hence this partial call for J. Turner to speak again. His view is really the very thing! It is just as it used to be. If T. has got it right the discussion is forever ended, and we have always been right, but did not know it; if we had, we should not have resorted to these puzzling arguments of Paul to prove that there is no Sabbath, to get clear of plain, bible doctrine!

As I have answered nearly all your arguments against the Sabbath and commandments, in my work on the Sabbath, and Waymarks, and lastly in my reply to the Advent Harbinger, under the head of the Four Pillar system, I shall be brief because I want to say a word upon another subject that you have named. You say, "to assume or infer that the Sabbath was commanded to men before the Exode from Egypt, is to walk as blind men. But at creation Adam's first day was the seventh day, or day on which God rested. Hence, if Adam kept Sabbath, he kept the first day, and then worked six days." Who said so? Not the bible. You would try to make out that Adam contradicted and disobeyed God's law, just as you have. Suppose you were born on Friday, the sixth day, would the next day, the seventh, be your first or second day? Your argument is not worth a straw; Adam's first day was Friday, the sixth day, and if he had been created the seventh day, that would have made no difference. How strange you talk! Because man should happen to come into life upon any other than the first day, then he must surely violate the Sabbath by doing his six days work first! This is in perfect keeping with "let every man be persuaded in his own mind," and not keep any. God rested the seventh day and blessed and sanctified it. Surely it is not so dangerous to follow God's example as it is to contradict and disobey him. Such as these are the blind men. [See first three pages of work on the Sabbath.]

Again, you say, "how long was the covenant or law of ten commandments to remain in force and effect, and answer Gal. iii, till Christ shall come." Under the third Pillar, I have answered this. The law of circumcision, and not the law of God, is Paul's whole argument here. The 17th verse shows the covenant is the one with Abraham, four hundred and thirty years before the law to Moses. There is not an intimation of the abolition of the law of commandments. Here it is the law of Abraham and Moses. Therefore it is right for the advocates of the seventh-day Sabbath to demand of you to prove a change of the Sabbath from the seventh to the first day; and the reason we demand it is, because we positively know you have none. You also say that the Apostles availed themselves of the opportunity to preach to the judaizing christians in their synagogues on the seventh day, at the same time keeping up the christian solemnity and worship on the first day. I say you cannot prove this. You cannot present a passage in the scriptures that shows that the disciples ever met together for worship, in the day time, on the first day of the week, and only once of an evening; and not one word about that being a holy day or a day for them to worship, but to break bread. But why do you want to prove this if all the commandments are abolished? The fact is, as soon as you leave the law of God, you are all adrift, with neither oar nor rudder, at the mercy of the tide. Again, you say "the ministration of the law is done away, is abolished." That is just what we say. Suppose you had ceased your ministration ten years ago, would that have abolished the Gospel? This is your reasoning, and it is the best argument you and others bring for the abolition of the commandments in 2d Cor. iii. There is nothing there but the ministration abolished, which no more affects the law of God, than the moving of your old sermons out of your house would affect the house.

Now will you just turn over your file to Nov. 4th, where you come out against J. P. M. Peck, about the sanctuary. As I have twice presented my view of the sanctuary's being in the heavens, I shall not stop here, only to say, that there is abundant bible proof for this view, and but one place for it, where Jesus, the High Priest is. But the one you advocate is first one thing and then another. Palestine, or Canaan, or Jerusalem, or mountains about Jerusalem; Mount Zion, and generally, the whole world. The reason for this is, because you have no proof of any certain place, after you leave Paul, in Heb. viii: 2. But you say, "I deny that it has been any thing like a general belief that the twenty-three hundred days ended in '44. There were a portion of the adventists that embraced, for a while, that theory. But they soon abandoned it, with the exception of a few, who have followed anything but the word of God and sound reason; and they now have no fellowship for, or connection with those who truly look for the cleansing of the sanctuary, at the end of the days; and we have as little fellowship for their teaching as they have for us and our view of the plain word of God. We know enough of the effect of that theory that teaches the 2300 days ended in '44, and scores of Shakers can tell you more even than we can."

Out of the great mass of advent believers in '44, I do not believe you knew of twenty that did not think the days were ended in '44. We will try to show, by-and-by, who have followed sound reason; and who have got "the plain word of God." You say you "know enough of the effect of that theory that teaches the 2300 days are ended." Allow me to tell you that you do not know so much about it as you think you do, or as you will wish you had. You are as much afloat here as you are on the subject of the Sabbath and commandments. That portion who abandoned the idea of the days being ended, of which you boast, are of those that organized and entered the state of the Laodocean church, "neither hot nor cold;" neither in one position nor yet in another; "always learning and never coming to the knowledge of (the present) truth." The ending of the 2300 days was the great burden of the advent teaching in '43 and '44; "then the sanctuary shall be cleansed." You will have it that this cannot be before the coming of the Lord, and you see he may come at any time; yes, now, by the first of January, as your Bible Advocate states. You have now heard something of the character of this J. Weston. He would have us believe that he was so full of the spirit of the Lord, that God had revealed to him that Jesus would come the 24th of December, or by the 1st of January. All good—we will publish it! What about the 2300 days, Br. W.? Oh, no matter, Jesus is coming now. H. H. Gross has refuted this time, but look at *him* last spring; the 1335 days must end the 18th day of April, and the resurrection, or they would not end under forty-five years. Well, he confessed that he was wrong in ever believing that they had ended in '44. Come, then, where will they end here? Oh, somewhere a little while before the 1335 days end in the spring of 1847. Well, time has passed on; out he comes again and says the Lord will come in the spring of 1848. Where will the 2300 and 1335 days end, friend Gross? Can't say—that is, he don't say—neither does J. Weston, and he does not correct him for this; it is only because the advent cannot be until spring. And here I will ask an opinion—that there is not a man in the whole advent ranks—(it seems to me that I will not even except you)—that can show that the Lord will come this winter or next spring. H. H. Gross is just as much mistaken in his calculation this coming spring, as he was the last. Now you may go on and call us what it seems to you good, we are confident that you have not got the present truth, neither have you had it since you have followed any thing but "*the word of God and sound reason.*" And this is the main reason why you cannot answer brother Fuller's important questions on THE OPEN BOOK OF REV. x: 2. It requires some one that has followed the truth, the present truth, nearer than you have, to reply to such questions, and *they* as surely involve the days as a cry at midnight brought us to the end of them. Do you not see how you are first blowing hot and then blowing cold? Six weeks ago, you said you knew enough of the effect of that theory that the *days* are ended. You say "all will see by reading the article, what are Br. F.'s views." That is, he is one that we have no fellowship for. But, you say, we hope that he and many others may be benefitted by a careful and prayerful investigation of some of the many questions he has asked. &c. &c. Now this is the right and only way to investigate. But if some one undertakes to follow your advice by the scripture, it would not amount to much, for we should expect to see you right out against them, for those that have rejected plain scripture, connected with experience, as you have, and ridiculed those who had faith in it, have but little hope now, since you have become an editor. We deeply lamented that you should have taken such a course; but we have seen since, that it required something more than common moral courage, for a shepherd to remain with the tried and tempted flock, when he sees that *all* his fellow shepherds were deserting them. The warnings you have had, have no doubt brought many solemn convictions to yours and their minds, or else we should not find you in this lukewarm state. Yes, you have been faithfully warned by your old, firm friends, not to come out with your Advocate; you have heard their voice, that two were enough to give the light on the doctrine of the advent, and they had hard work to get along. But no, your paper was going to take different ground, in some things! In one respect, it has shown pretty clearly, as the scriptures fully demonstrate, that "the dead know not any thing;" and allow me here to tell you, if you go on with your no-law-of-God and no-commandment system, and continue to reject the clear fulfillment of prophecy, in our past experience, you will as clearly prove that you know but a very *little* more. But after all you have said and done, you are following hard on in the track—the same old deep-cut rut, made by your predecessors. Pharaoh's host like, the ruts so deep you can neither back nor turn out; but on you drive after them, thinking, no doubt, that you are going to accomplish something for God and his cause. The only way that I can see for you to do that, will be, either to abandon your load, or shift the tongue of your chariot on the opposite end, drive back with all speed, and get into the highway of the Waymarks and high heaps, that you so wilfully abandoned more than three years ago.

The Saviour's admonition to the Philadelphia state of the church, which was forming in '43 and '44, was to hold fast that which we had—and he would "write upon us his new name." This is what we are endeavoring to do; and when we see you doing the opposite, we know you are wrong. You quote Paul to the Hebrews, viii: 10, "Saith the Lord I will put my laws into their mind and write them in their hearts." Whose hearts? Answer—the house of Israel; of course, all of God's people. What is this done for? Answer—that he may be our God and we may know him and be his people. Can you tell your no-law no-commandment readers which law of God Paul meant? Whether it was the one you say he abolished in Col., Gal., Cor. and Romans, or was it another code of laws which he had made for our purpose, and then hid them from us. If you know in what book, or chapter, or verse they are in the bible, I beseech you to let us know immediately, for I see by John's visions in the Rev. that in the last days there certainly will be a company keeping them, and the Devil will persecute them for it; but they will eventually be saved, and enter the city. Rev. xii: 17; xiv: 12; xxii: 14. And finally, if you cannot find any others than those which God gave by his own mouth and wrote with his own finger on Mount Sinai, more than 3300 years since, the same which Jesus confirmed to us more than 1800 years ago with his Gospel, won't you make that known by publicly confessing that it is impossible for you to tell what other object God had in view than our keeping these same laws; and that you had, contrary to the direct teachings of God, derided both his law and his willing, obedient children. Don't tell us that this law is the "*law* of *Christ* or the *law* of *grace*," or any other name unless you can show us how many commandments they contain, because James has told us "if we fail in one we are guilty of the whole." Jesus never gave but one commandment.

---

P. S. As I predicted on your second page, J. Turner's piece has come. The *child* is fairly born, and you have fallen in love with it. Now brethren, just haul down all your other colors, J. Turner has got the very thing! The first day of the week is the seventh-day Sabbath! We have always been right, but we never knew it till now! Thanks to J. Turner for confounding the whole world, and now no more about this much vexed question! "We shall fill our paper mostly with other matter for the future." The wind has favored us and we have made a first rate tack to windward, and now we can breathe much freer seeing our enemies are under our lee. Hear what he says? "We supposed and still do suppose that Barnabas had reference to a class well known to the adventists in Connecticut and Massachusetts, who went into the shut door, and staid in, and almost every other door but the true one into the sheepfold, and *many* of which became great sticklers for the seventh day." &c. Now he goes on and speaks in high praise of those who have been writing for the Sabbath—*they* are consistent Christians, &c. And now, says he, "we must all be *exceedingly* careful how we *write* and *speak*; the enemy seeks to devour us, and one of his most artful wiles is to divide the saints by *dark insinuations, evil speaking,* and *jealousies,*" &c.—See Bible Advocate, Dec. 30th, p. 160. Why this caution after the above unsparing epithets; are you afraid that some of these misguided, mistaken people will get into your open door? If they should happen to, and confess that they were wrong in believing in the shut door, no matter how many others they had been guilty of entering into what you call almost every door, they would immediately become consistent Christians! Out of hundreds who have crawled into your open door and made such confessions, causing the hypocrites and unbelievers to rejoice, and the hearts of the righteous to be sad, &c., I will just name a few: J. and C. Pearsons, F. G. Brown, of wonderful memory; and now a few Sabbath keepers: W. M. Ingham, John Howell, of vascillating memory, and J. Turner, your fellow laborer. Well, you are not so far to windward as you think for; here comes another head flaw, that will drive you down on that lee shore again, where you may see the awful havoc you have made of those who are following in your wake. See them dashing there upon the rocks and into those overwhelming breakers! Your whirlwind of doctrine has utterly dismantled them, and their cry for help is unavailing! and unless you put forth some more strenuous efforts to avoid these dangerous seas, you will never get off from this lee shore, while under these deceitful and flattering winds of doctrine.

Again he says—"We take the liberty to add, that Br. T.'s article is IRREFUTABLE, and that we are now observing the Sabbath of the Lord our God, and not the Jewish, nor a Pagan Sabbath." Where is he now? Does he mean that J. T.'s Sabbath is "the Sabbath of the Lord our God?" He has always insisted, in his former articles, that "the Sabbath of the Lord our God," *was* the Jewish Sabbath. There is but one named in the bible. If this what he calls "the plain word of the Lord," I doubt whether any one will understand him.

He says further—"If Friday was the sixth day—every transaction on the day of our Lord's crucifixion is involved in utter confusion—and the law of types in a like failure, and makes it an impossibility for the Sabbath of the Lord our God to be kept the next day, for this [*wise*] reason, that it was a feast day"! and quotes John xix: 31, again and again, for positive proof. I wonder if he can tell how, and when, and where the Jews lost that day, since the crucifixion, and where is the history to show that they did really pass over the seventh-day Sabbath and keep the first day for the Sabbath? I have already answered this in J. Turner's article; there you will see the reason why John called this "an high day." Now, as he has spoken of the law of types, I ask where is the chapter and verse in the bible in which the Jews were ever forbidden to hold a feast, when it fell on the seventh-day Sabbath? for, as I before stated, this always did occur every year. Besides this Jewish feast was an holy convocation; no servile work was to be done on this day. This was always continued seven days, and the last day was like the first. Lev. xxiii: 6-8. Now then, all that they did on these feast Sabbaths, was to worship God by their offerings. You see that on God's holy seventh-day Sabbath, [see J. T.'s article,] they always offered four lambs; therefore, whenever the other Sabbaths, or holy convocations fell on the seventh day, they were equally observed, as is positively proved by the direction of God in the 37th and 38th verses of this same chapter, "every thing upon his day besides the Sabbaths of the Lord," &c. Now see—here are seven holy convocations, Sabbath feasts named in this chapter, which the Jews were required to keep besides the weekly seventh-day Sabbath, and when their feasts fell on the holy Sabbath of the Lord, all the extra labor was in offering to God the extra bullocks, lambs &c. Do let me entreat you, before you further expose yourself, to read in connection with this, the twenty-eighth and twenty-ninth chapter of Numbers, for here you will find every identical thing specified: therefore, when one of these seven holy convocation days of every year came on the weekly Sabbath, it was of more importance, inasmuch that they had more offerings to make to God, and hence John or any one else, might call it "an high day;" but none the less holy, any more than for us, instead of assembling together on the Sabbath, in our several places for worship, to have a general conference meeting in Boston, to continue over the Sabbath.

But J. Turner, instead of overthrowing history, as he promised he should, is exulting, and says, "unless I utterly misapprehend the technical veracity of Christ and his apostles, *I have the argument* by their concurrent testimony." In his Note 3, he says, "But if the day that followed the crucifixion was the seventh-day Sabbath, it could not be said that the Sabbath drew on, for it was even then *began*. It commenced at evening, at the same time the pascal lamb was slain in the law, at which time according to the record, Jesus expired."

Now, I say, this is not true, and he or the editor who published it, knows it to be so. I presume that both of them have stated in their preaching, again and again, that Jesus expired on the cross at the ninth hour, as the Evangelists testify, which was at three o'clock in the afternoon, and three hours before the Sabbath commenced. If he can assert such positive falsehoods as these, and others which I have stated, to prove what never has, nor never will take place, and at the same time have multitudes crying "amen!" "that's true!" &c., it is no wonder he can "set *as calm as heaven!*"

But I have one other proof to offer, which will destroy their whole foundation. I had overlooked it in the multitude of texts that had come up here, but God in answer to our prayers, both in our closet and at meetings, for wisdom to guide us in giving the *present truth* to the little flock in this work, at this important crisis, has so directed that I may have it in time to put into this Postscript, just as it is going to press. [I could not see before why it was that the printer could not get his promised help, in order to proceed faster with this work. I see it now—it is all in God's own wise way. He was not willing, (as it now appears to me,) that my work should come out to check or disturb you, until you began to settle somewhere on this subject.] The proof then, I transcribe from a letter received from Br. JAMES WHITE, dated Topsham, Me. January 2d, 1848. Here it is:

> "The plain, simple truth in regard to the holy Sabbath flows out from the blessed bible in one clear, strait channel; while erroneous views are fated to run crooked and devour themselves. I think that those who are not fully settled as to what day of the week is the seventh or Sabbath, would do well to refer to the type, in Lev. xxii: 5-21. Here are three types which were fulfilled at the time of the first advent. Every adventist in the land once believed that these types were exactly fulfilled as to time. The paschal lamb was slain on the 14th day of the first

month. So was Jesus crucified on the 14th day of the first month. The handful of the first fruits of the harvest was waved before the Lord on the 16th of the first month; so was Jesus the first fruits of the resurrection, raised from the tomb the 16th of the first month. [See 1st Cor. xv: 20.] Now if the resurrection day, which was the first day of the week, was the 16th of the first month, then it follows that the 14th of the first month when Jesus was crucified, which was Friday, was the sixth day of the week; Saturday, the seventh day or Sabbath, and Sunday, the first day of the week.

"St. Paul preached that Christ would rise the third day, according to the scriptures. He certainly could refer to no other scripture but the type. Our Lord, while preaching the resurrection to the two, on their way to Emmeas, began at Moses. So we are not on forbidden ground when we go there also, to prove that he arose on the third day.—See Luke xxiv: 27, 44-46. Jesus came not to break, but to fulfill every jot and tittle of the law— therefore he arose Sunday, the 16th day of the first month, which harmonizes with the joint testimony of the Apostles and Christ himself, that he arose on the third day."

Other brethren, (in reference to J. Turner's article,) from Canandaigua, N. Y. and Dorchester, Mass. have also, about this same time, referred us to this strong hold, for which we thank them and praise the Lord for this light, that forever settles the question. A most striking proof of the *unity* of the saints in their patience, (Rev. xiv: 12,) no matter where located, though hundreds and thousands of miles apart, they are one on this question. This is as we now understand the Sabbath of the Lord our God, to be the rallying point of all those who are truly looking for the speedy coming of Jesus. Whosoever, therefore, shall attempt to destroy or *displace* God's holy Sabbath, will have to pass the examination of the host. Paul to the Corinthians, 5th chapter and seventh verse, says, "For even Christ our passover is sacrificed for us." How? Answer—expired on Friday, the 14th day of the first month, at 3 o'clock, P. M., in exact fulfillment of the type by Moses, in Exo. xii: 6, 11-14, continued for 1670 years. He rested from *all* his works only one twenty-four hour day, and that was God's holy day. Paul tells the Romans that "he was raised again for our justification." iv: 25; and the Corinthians "that he is risen and become the first fruits of them that slept." 1st Cor. xv: 20; and Col. i: 18, "first born from the dead." Again, "should be the *first* that should rise from the dead."

Acts xxvi: 23. John says, "The first begotten of the dead." He arose on Sunday morning, the first day of the week, before sunrise—say about 5 A. M.—having been dead about thirty-eight hours. Thus he fulfilled the type in Lev. xxiii: 10-11 verses—the first fruits of the harvest, the handful of barley, called the wafe sheaf, which was waved by the priest, with the offering of a lamb, [emblem of Christ,] as first fruits of the resurrection, on the morrow after the Sabbath—the 16th of the first month—the Sabbath, or feast day, always being on the 15th of the same month. Then, from the 14th, at 3 P. M. to the 16th, at about 6 P. M. is but thirty-eight hours, *two* whole nights, (not three,) one whole day, a part of Friday and a part of Sunday. "Thus it behoved Christ to suffer and to rise from the dead the *third day.*" This is his own testimony a few hours after his resurrection; also a few hours after the offering of the wafe sheaf. If this can be overthrown then can also the time of his crucifixion. The chaotic confusion that you would make about this great feast day which always followed the passover, is answered here. It so happened in the order of time to come on God's holy Sabbath; and that God so ordered it that Christ should rest from all his works on his holy day, was without doubt, to fulfill some glorious event yet to come.

Now, friend Timothy, if you will not reverence God's holy Sabbath and commandments according to the clear precept, do you let them alone, if you do not want a worse thing to befal you, for just so sure as you fight against them they will destroy you. This beating the air, is some like daubing with untempered mortar; you cannot make any of it stay put. If I were in your place, I should a great deal rather have been fast asleep than to be caught in such heaven-daring business—fighting against God! This looks like *"following anything but* 'the word of God and sound reason.'"

During '43 and '44, Dowling, Stewart, Colver, Chase, Bush and others, took their stand against William Miller and his brethren, to demolish Daniel's vision of the 2300 days. You remember that no two of these agreed, but each started upon a theory of his own; but God's children were united and on the one point, and therefore triumphed over them all. Now you leading men are acting the drama over again, with regard to the Sabbath and commandments of God. See how it looks; William Miller believes the first day is the Sabbath; J. V. Himes believes in selecting any day, just as you are persuaded, but still *calls the first the Sabbath*; Joseph Marsh is not particular, don't believe there is either law, Sabbath or commandments—says we are under the law of grace; but still he will have it, that Sunday is the Sabbath! you say the first day is the seventh of the Lord our God, but it is not the Jewish Sabbath,—that is; the one which is in the decalogue. It is something new—I don't understand you; don't think you can make your brethren understand it, either. J. Turner says the first day is the true seventh-day Sabbath! D. B. Wait says the commandments are right, but the first day is the true seventh-day. Barnabas says "the Jews were right in killing our Lord for a notorious Sabbath breaker, if he did not abolish all the law when he commenced his ministry," three years before he abolished Moses' law. Up starts another mighty man, G. Needham, and says God told him that the commandments were all abolished in 2d Corinthians, chapter 3d. And a great portion of your flattering readers are flying like Mother Cary's Chickens[2] to get into your WAKE to pick up the crumbs! Don't smile, gentle reader, the picture is not overdrawn. These are some of the principal leaders in the second advent; they will tell you to your face that they have renounced all sectarian creeds and formulas, and believe every word of God. Now the *"great sticklers for the seventh day,"* are all united on the Sabbath and commandments; they believe God, if they keep his Sabbath, that they shall be sanctified and ride upon the high places of the earth.—Ezekiel and Isaiah. They believe Jesus, that the law and the prophets hang upon the commandments, and that the keeping of them will give eternal life and great esteem in the reign of heaven. This carries them beyond the Jewish, Gospel, and all other dispensations. See also Rev. xxii: 14. They believe the holy Apostles, Paul, John and James—that "the law is holy, and the commandments holy, just and good." "Here are they [Jan. 1848] that keep the commandments of God and the faith of Jesus." Rev. xiv: 12. "If we keep the whole law and yet offend in one point, we are guilty of all." They feel perfectly secure in following such leaders, and they understand that though you be ever so moral in regard to  the nine commandments, you fail in the fourth, the Sabbath. They believe this to be the "plain word of the Lord," and on this Sabbath question they will all be united, waiting for Jesus. And just so sure as the first class of expositors were overthrown by rejecting the sure word, just so sure you will be overwhelmed in utter confusion that oppose God's holy Sabbath and commandments, and your case is now hanging in awful suspense. O Lord, let the clear light shine.

A word more—as your wonderful prototype has also threatened to unsettle the world with respect to the history of the seventh-day Sabbath. If he proceeds with it as he has with the unerring word of God, our minds will have to be remodelled, to believe with him. If any of the little flock feel desirous of spending an hour in looking into this subject, I would recommend them to send to the New York Sabbath Tract Society, and purchase Sabbath tract No. 4, vol. 1, 48 pages. This will save the labor of poring over Roman and English history, or of following the sophistical arguments of the blind leading the blind. Much reliance is placed upon the history of the "early fathers," so called, who succeeded the Apostles, to settle the question. We ought to remember that these were uninspired men, and we do not know even so much about their characters, as we do of the uninspired fathers of the last century, whose teaching led us all into Babylon. If the true history of the advent doctrine from 1842 to the autumn of 1844, had, with the subsequent events in our history up to 1848, been published

1800 years ago from the Advent Heralds, and their conductors had been called the fathers—it would have puzzled all the wise heads in Christendom, in this age, to have expounded their meaning; for we see it requires all the energies of the human mind to trace their crooked tracks, even when right before us. For this reason, I have said but little about history; my whole and entire reliance being upon the inspired word of the living God. This, we are told, will make us *"perfect* and *entire—wanting nothing."*—2d Tim. iii: 17.

If what I have and may here present in this work will not stand the test of what we have seen and felt ourselves—fulfilling the clear word of God in these last days, then I shall fail in my object of comforting and strengthening the flock of God. I fully believe in history, when all deductions are fully allowed.

# Past And Present Experience.

To William Miller,

*Dear Sir*,—The time was, when all second advent believers were dear to you, and they called you father and brother Miller. Alas, how changed the scene is now! Jesus says "whosoever shall do the will of my Father which is in heaven, the same is my brother and sister and mother." They can't believe that you are doing the will of God, as you once was, though they cannot help loving and venerating your name for the great light which you have given— because you are wounding their feelings by calling them Fanatics, Door-Shutters, and almost any thing but honest people, to destroy all their reputation and christian fellowship, and make them feel if possible, that they are worse than the heathen. In this way you have weaned their affection from you, and when you give them an exposition of God's word now, they doubt: say they, he first gave us the light, and we rallied to his standard, because it agreed with the scriptures—but when we were come to the most trying and toilsome part of our journey then he forsook us and joined in with the shepherds and those of like faith, to berate us. But we soon learnt from the prophets that there would be a people in the last days, answering this description, that God had promised to save, called *Outcasts*!—Jer. xxx: 17; Psl. cxlvii: 2. Now you are encouraging these same deniers of our faith to be *peaceable*; for—say you—we shall soon get into the kingdom of God. Methinks if we should all meet there under existing circumstances, there would be a great deal of confessing before we could be reconciled to listen to each other's joys. But it will not be so; if you and your brethren, and the *outcasts* too, are saved, then I predict that we shall have to stay here until a perfect reconciliation takes place. When that will be, I cannot tell, for in my judgment the gulf between us has been widening for the last three years. Now, I prefer to remain on that side of it with the *Outcasts*, for they have the promise that they shall be gathered. When we made our sacrifice during a cry at midnight, we considered and were fully persuaded that we were doing our last work, and surely that would *be done the best of any work*. Then of course we had no right whatever to take back the sacrifices we then made, and rob God. We were fully aware that our disappointments would not change our course, for if we were ever saved it must be by our onward course. But those with whom you were associated sounded the retreat, and all that did not follow in their train have been subject to your unsparing epithets.

If you knew as much about this afflicted and torn people, (whom you have been the instrument in leading out into the Philadelphia state of the church, and then leaving and driving them from you,) as I do, you would shudder to appear before Him who has promised to be a Father to them and keep them. The principal cause of many offences which they committed were from bad teachers and teaching. You have a sample here in this work. (We have no wish, *neither do we uphold* any one who does not follow the teachings of the sure word.) I think you have listened too much to them.

If I could just take you with me to some of the stopping places of these people, and show you their scanty wood piles at this inclement season of the year, and then to the barrels which once held their beef, pork and flour, together with the scanty subsistence they now have, and with no earthly prospect of another supply, only as their trust is in the living God, in whom they had committed their all, because of their honest sacrifice and anxious waiting for their coming Lord; turned out of their former employment and reproached for keeping God's holy Sabbath day; whipped by cruel, unmerciful men for shouting the praises of their God and king, and still persevering in their faith, &c. And then, for a contrast, to step on board the cars and be rolled away to your own comfortable and commodious house, with well stocked barn  and granaries, beef and pork barrels—the produce of your own valuable farm—with all things that heart could wish for, and set down by your comfortable fire with your family, (all believers with you in the coming of Jesus,) and recount to them the strange scenes you had witnessed among an afflicted people, who once listened with anxiety and delight to every word you had to say about the second coming of Jesus, and they were so delighted with this, to them, joyful news, that they wanted to hear about it all the time. We may imagine your conversation to proceed somewhat in the following strain:

"You remember how elder Himes used to insist on my going with him from city to city, and from state to state, because of the people's anxiety to hear me preach about the coming of Christ in 1843 and '44."

"Yes, father, I remember it well—for when I was with you it seemed as though the people were hardly willing to let us come home and rest a little while."

"I know it, my son, and I used to think that God never would have sustained me in such continued and incessant labors as I was then called to perform, if it were not his cause. Why, when I saw the wonderful effect that it produced on backsliders and sinners, in bringing them to God, and the glow of joy that lit up in the countenances of God's honest, believing children, and how they hung upon every word; and then the contrary effect, when some of their learned ministers raised their objections—I said I know this is God's cause, and as it rolled on through that cry at midnight, down to its closing scene, you all remember with what joy and glory I was filled, and how I publicly declared my faith, and stated that 'I might be called a FANATIC, but, I said, call me what you please, Christ will come,' &c. Well, these singular people are some of the very ones that used to hang on my words and others, who preached to them of this doctrine. And during this cry at midnight they made a sacrifice of all they had—(some of them were almost as well off as *we are*, and some were poor,)—but they offered what they had, and that was all that was required."

"Grandfather, what makes them poor now that had something then? You know the Saviour didn't come then, as you said he would, and that is more than three years ago."

"Well, they thought it would be contrary to scripture to take back their sacrifice, and so many of them have made no improvements on their farms, nor their buildings,—no, they have not even made *stone walls*! Some of them sold what they had, and have been trying to help the poorer ones, because they said they still believed that Christ was coming, and they would not need it. For instance, they believe what Luke has recorded in his xii: 33—'Sell your goods and give alms; lay not up treasure on the earth,'—they think this must be understood literally! and they have gone off into many strange notions, believing the door is shut, &c. &c."

"Well, how do they appear, father?"

"They do not seem to be, in the least, alarmed at poverty; they are expecting soon to be delivered and made heirs with Jesus, to an incorruptible inheritance that will abide forever. I could get along with many points in their faith, and believe them honest, if they did not make them tests for us; and because we do not believe in the great work that was wrought in the past, and the present truths that they advocate, they have no charity for us. They say we have backslidden and gone into a cold lukewarm Laodocean state of the church."

"Well, father, I believe there is a great deal of truth in their statements, for there certainly is a wonderful difference in our camp and conference meetings, to what there used to be, for if any one shouts glory to God, now, as they used to in '43 and '44, it seems as if the whole meeting was agitated, until it is ascertained that it is one of the deluded ones, it seems as though they hardly dare say amen, either because they do not believe what you say, or for fear they shall be called *fanatics*. You know how they tried you and how hard you talked to them about it in the conference in Boston, last spring. You thought it was because they had no religion. And then the camp meeting too, at Lake Champlain; I suppose the most of them thought that you were going to prove that the door was shut, and that the past was true; and a good many of them might still have thought so, if elder Marsh had not taken it up and called forth your explanation, in his paper of Sept 28th. For my part, I don't really understand all these things—that as soon as you begin to advocate the past truths in any of our meetings, these editors are either writing or visiting you to explain it more fully in their papers, and then neither party seems to be satisfied. If I were you, I would take a strait-forward course, and try to please God, if I could not any one else."

"Well, my son, you know that these two editors have stood by me ever since 1842, and as for elder Himes, he has stood by me and been my warm and fast friend all these last seven years of joy and trials, and I cannot separate from him. No, I have told him that I would sustain him and his paper if I had to carry down our *potatoes to Boston,* to raise the means. You see I must stand by him, and he and brother Marsh will defend and justify my course and views of bible doctrine; and defend my character from the aspersions of my enemies, and gladly publish any thing I have to say against the *Door Shutters,* &c."

"Yes, yes—I know all that, father, but some how or other, these things do not look right. You began with a strait-forward bible course, and it cut like a sword with two edges, and that is the reason why these door shutters, &c., as you call them, believed your testimony, and they think there is just as much edge to the sword now as there ever was. However, you have studied the bible much more than I have, therefore I shall not dispute you, but I cannot see that this people, whom you have been to visit, are so much out of the way for venturing to go forward, after *your clear directions to them,* soon after the cry at midnight."

But it may be said that these are what are termed the "No-work Folks." No sir, they do not belong to that class, although their views are, in most all other respects, similar. You have been told—or, I have—by one of your traveling lecturers, that there were but twenty-five of them, all told. He said they were proclaiming that they were all that would be saved at the second advent. We have no such view. We believe, what I shall attempt to prove by-and-by, that there will be 144,000 saved at the coming of Jesus. Furthermore, we believe that the same commandment which teaches us to keep the seventh-day Sabbath, also teaches that we may labor the other six days for just as much as we comfortably need; more than that would counteract the direction of Jesus, viz. "Lay not up for yourselves treasures on the earth," &c. This is all right, for our faith teaches us we do not need it. If we hoard up what we have got, it certainly is not selling and giving alms. My opinion is, that this is now to be made clear, and that God's people will be absolutely afraid to be found with a surplus treasure here, when Christ comes. As the keeping of the fourth commandment, in its true scriptural sense, carries us to the gates of the city, so our laboring honestly for what we immediately want, also carries us to that point. But we have no controversy with those who honestly and sincerely live to God without laboring; though they tell us that they have no charity for us, still we believe if they honestly live out their faith God will not condemn them for not working six days.

Your explanation respecting the time that Christ might, or has, began to reign, to prove that you had no connection or fellowship with *"door shutters"* or their views, is the most enigmatical of all your ideas, since 1845. I refer to your letter in the Advent Harbinger of Sept. 28th. It is endorsed by the editor, and also by the Advent Herald, in justifying the ground you took—and grew out of a report that elder S. Hall of Bangor, made from your conversation and preaching at the Champlain camp meeting. I reported what I heard, and it was therefore stated that I was present. This you could have contradicted, but the editor has since acknowledged his mis-statement. S. Hall is an entire stranger to me. I have written him two letters on the subject, without reply. But it is your own written statement that so puzzles me. You give from 1815 to 1847, thirty-two years, for Michael in Dan. xii: 1, to stand up to reign, and you further say it might have been at the end of the 2300 days. This is the first intimation I have had, since you took your stand against us, that you believed the days ended; but the forty-five years latitude for Christ to begin to reign, and your anathemas at those who believe the door is shut, is as incomprehensible to me as Swedenbourgenism—J. Marsh's explained exposition of Nov. 9th, to the contrary notwithstanding. As I have already given my views about the time when Christ began to reign, in *Way Marks*, page 35 and onward, I may not say much here. Have the 2300 days really ended then, and nothing to *mark* their end? This was the burthen of your cry. It was also the prophets, and one of them said it should speak and not lie. Then, of course, it would not come silently; but the wise would understand when it did end. You reply, I suppose, according to the 11th chapter of Revelations, from which you was speaking, that the seventh trumpet had began to sound; but was there nothing else connected with the ending of the 2300 days? Yes—the third wo, because that belongs to the seventh trumpet; see viii: 13. Now the 10th chapter, 7th verse, shows us that when this seventh trumpet begins to sound, the Mystery of God should be finished. Oh, you say, that's the old story of 1845. Yes sir, and more than seventeen hundred years beyond that. Here is your trouble; but the most of your hearers, though they may listen with delight to you, yet they preach that the seventh trumpet does not sound until Christ comes to raise the dead. You ought to correct them here, for they are certainly in the dark; Christ is not the seventh messenger.

Besides, if Christ has began to reign as you say, over the nations, he has, according to your showing in Daniel xii: 1, changed his position. If so, how can he be in the mediatorial seat? His leaving that finishes the Mystery, and that forever *shuts the door*, unless you or some one else can prove that he leaves this work over the nations, and goes back again to finish what he left undone.

Now, who is the fanatic here? You cannot make all this work in harmony—it is impossible; besides, you call us spiritualizers, because of our view of the Bridegroom. If we are, pray what are you? and how did you find out that Christ had changed his position, even twenty years ago? or when the 2300 days ended, somewhere since 1843? It really appears to me, that if *we* had put forth such a view, that we should have been pronounced crazy! and yet your two editors will patch it all up, and throw all the stigma upon us, forsooth, because they think we shall claim you as an *Outcast!* Their fears are unnecessary—we have no claim to such views; they would only disturb our ranks. We believe that the seventh trumpet began to sound on the first day of the seventh month. Then the Mystery was finished, and the third wo came. The virgins in the parable, were divided—some went after oil. On the tenth day of the seventh month is the day of atonement. At this point in 1841, in the order of the fulfillment of the types in Leviticus and New Testament testimony, (which we have referred to in the *Way Marks*) Jesus received his Bride and the kingdoms of this world, and entered the Holy of Holies as our Great High Priest, and commenced the cleansing of the Sanctuary. Why? Because here the 2300 days ended:—*The appointed time.* At this point too, commenced the trial of God's people. Surely you never can forget this, until the trial ends; and that cannot end in accordance with the type, until our Great High Priest and King has finished the cleansing of the Sanctuary, the New Jerusalem, and it is made holy; see Joel iii: 17. Now follow the type and Bible testimony, and it is positively clear that Jesus changes his position from the daily ministration to the most holy place, just as certainly as Aaron did. Here then, in short, is where we prove the Bridegroom come to the Marriage, and the door shut, in the parable of Matt. xxv, and in the types. If it does not prove this in our past history, and that we are now waiting for our coming king, then these types are superfluous. We do not believe that Michael stands up, as you have stated, until he has accomplished what is above stated. We cannot possibly see how he can begin to reign over the nations as king, while he is in the most holy place, cleansing the Sanctuary, and the saints being perfected for the blessing when he lays aside his priestly robes and takes the sickle, as in Rev. xiv: 14; and God speaks, as in Joel iii: 16. If what you have stated, had been even approbated in Oct. 1844, it would have thrown the whole harmony of the scriptures, in our past history, into confusion. As I have said, I will here repeat it, that unless you follow the Bible rule as I have stated here and in the *Way Marks*, you never can harmonize the scriptures with the *past* nor *present*; and I think I shall make it plainer still, before I lay down my pen.

One thing more: Much derision is made about those of our company that have joined the Shakers. I say it is a shame to them first, to have preached in clearly and distinctly the speedy coming of our Lord Jesus Christ *personally* to gather his saints—and then to go and join the Shakers in their faith, that he

(Jesus) came spiritually in their Mother, Ann Lee, more than seventy years ago. This, without doubt in my mind, is owing to their previous teaching and belief in a doctrine called the *trinity*. How can you find fault with their faith while you are teaching the very essence of that never—no never to be understood, doctrine? For their comfort and faith, and of course your own, you say *"Christ is God, and God is love."* As you have given no explanation, we take it to come from you as a literal exposition of the word; and although the editor of the Herald, of Dec 4th, endeavors to justify you in your published view of the Unity in 1842, and thinks he has made it clear that you have not changed your views on this subject, just as he is in the habit of doing without your knowledge, but still you have not confirmed it, and your having changed your views once at least since 1844, leaves us in doubt about the editor's remarks. We ask, then, where you find this passage, and if ever love was seen; and if that is what we are looking for from heaven, to come the second time? If so, how will it look, and where is the scripture that describes it? It seems to me that the shakers have a better claim to you than we have.

We believe that Peter and his master settled this question beyond controversy, Matt. xvi: 13-19; and I cannot see why Daniel and John has not fully confirmed that Christ is the Son, and, not God the Father. How could Daniel explain his vision of the 7th chapter, if "Christ was God." Here he sees one "like the Son (and it cannot be proved that it was any other person) of man, and there was given him Dominion, and Glory, and a kingdom;" by the ancient of days. Then John describes one seated on a throne with a book in his right hand, and he distinctly saw Jesus come up to the throne and take the book out of the hand of him that sat thereon. Now if it is possible to make these two entirely different transactions appear in one person, then I could believe your text if I could believe that God died and was buried instead of Jesus, and that Paul was mistaken when he said. "Now the God of peace that *brought again* from the *dead our Lord Jesus* that great shepherd of the sheep" &c., and that Jesus also did not mean what he said when he asserted that he came from God, and was going to God, &c. &c.; and much more, if necessary, to prove the utter absurdity of such a faith. Without going any further, we say that one of two things is certainly clear, that the doctrine of the second advent, which you, and your adherents promulgated down to Oct. 1844, was positively wrong, if you *now* are right. We believe it was right and approved of God and therefore we fully believe that we are in the right road still, but we have nothing to boast of; our track has been made dark by your opposition, but still we have travelled on, believing that light is sown for the righteous, and we have realized it; to God be all the praise. If you and your adherents could have turned us into your course, you would. We rejoice that we are in the furnace. Our deluded course, as it is termed, arises from three things that we practice: First, we are called Judaizers, because we keep the Sabbath according to the commandment; our reasons for it, are with you.

We say further that God set us the example, as he has the whole world. Jesus and the apostles followed, and so do we. Second, because we wash one another's feet, here we have the plain and positive teaching and example of Jesus: "If I, then, the master and the teacher, have washed your feet.—Happy are ye who know these things provided ye PRACTICE them."—[Camp. trans.]—John xiii. Third, that we practice kissing.—Here we have the teaching, of the great apostle to the Gentiles, to churches and households and every individual believer in Christ Jesus; see Rom. xvi: 3, 6, 12-16; 1st Thes. v: 26, "Greet all the brethren with a holy kiss;" Phil. iv: 21. "Salute every saint in Christ Jesus." Now I do not say but here is dangerous ground, and no doubt many have fallen, because they could not stand the test, as Paul's brethren could not the communion; but did Paul advise them to give it up because some had lost their lives for it? No! Well, then, the rule is the same with us, not to yield because some have spiritually died. It is a test of our fellowship for one another, and we may just as well be ashamed of the teachings of the bible as to be ashamed or afraid to practice what is clearly taught. Our course is onward; we leave you say what you please of us. We very clearly see if we persevere in this course, that it will lead us to immortality.

---

P. S. Some days after writing the above, an acquaintance of mine loaned me the Advent Herald of Jan. 8th, 1848, to read the remarkable dream, which you had in November last. I am glad that the Lord comforted you by giving you this dream. Since I have read it, I do feel a hope that the Lord will yet save you from the delusive snare into which your pretended friends seemed to have drawn you. Joel's prophecy, quoted by Peter, at the Pentecost, respecting dreams and visions of the last days, are not, in my view, fulfilled; nor cannot be, unless it can be proved that the *last* days are past. I fully believe that God warns and instructs his children in various ways, when deep sleep is fallen upon them. There certainly are some very remarkable cases on record in the Bible, and I as much believe them, as other portions of his word.

It seemed to me that I could see some of the outlines of this dream; for instance, the "curiously wrought casket, filled with all sorts and sizes of jewels, diamonds, precious stones, and gold and silver coin of every dimension and value, beautifully arranged in their several places in the casket." These, I think, clearly represent the special treasure, the jewels of the Lord of hosts, that are now being made up in this day of trial, as saith Malachi; brought out and made manifest by the second advent doctrine, which you began to give to the world some few years ago. Many of them, at that time, bound down by the sectarian creeds and formulas in Babylon, were aroused and won away by the soul-stirring doctrine of the coming of Christ, in 1843 and '44. No wonder that your friends, who then gathered around you, shouted for joy when they began critically and earnestly to examine the curiously wrought casket, (the word of God,) and to see, the more they examined and expounded, the more the diamonds and jewels increased in splendor, brilliancy and numbers, (converts from the churches and the world,) and scattering all over the land, (the centre table,) and in a few years throughout the world, every nation, kindred, tongue and people, (all over the floor and furniture.) By this time the flying messengers in Rev. xiv, began to draw these jewels out into a clear place by themselves, (the Philadelphia state of the church,) saying, behold, the Bridegroom cometh, go ye out to meet him! As soon as the disapointment came in Oct. 1844, then your counterfeit coin and immense quantities of spurious jewels (hypocrites and unbelievers) were seen as you saw, scattered among the genuine. Here you felt the great responsibility of the doctrine you had been propogating, and proclaimed that our work for the world was done, and you was grieved to see that so few of the great multitude which had appeared delighted with your doctrine, really believed it. Hence you became "vexed in your very soul, and began to use physical force to *push them out.*" Here, I think is where you changed your views and course, in the spring of 1845, and united with those that have been increasing three to one, as you saw, bringing in dirt, and sand, and shavings and all manner of rubbish and covered up both the genuine and false jewels and diamonds, &c. These I think represent the false doctrine, since 1844, mixed up with almost every thing, and from every where, calling the honest and confiding children of God almost any thing but their true names; thus covering them up with, as you saw, dirt, sand, shavings, and rubbish of all kinds; at the same time so covering up also the spurious coin, (false teachers) that nothing of them, or of that beauty and glory that was so apparent a little while since, can now as it were, be seen, breaking in pieces your casket (the word of God) and trampling it also under foot. Just look at the Sabbath controversy, for one item, and the daubing with untempered mortar, this all absorbing subject of Christ coming to Judgment, and compare it with Ezek. xxxiv chapter, particularly the 21, 22 and 31st verses, and surely it will be admitted that "the Dream is certain and the interpretation thereof sure."

And whereas thou sawest a man enter the room with a dirt brush and open the windows to cleanse it of its filthiness at which time all the people passed out. The spurious coins also arose and passed out of the windows. The room was then cleansed of all its rubbish. All the genuine diamonds, precious coin and jewels, even to those not larger than the point of a pin, were collected, and beautifully arranged in another casket, which, when the man called you to look into, caused you to shout with very joy.

"Know therefore and understand;" that in *this day* of atonement, while our Great High Priest is cleansing the sanctuary, (blotting out his people's sins,) preparing his jewels (Mal. iii: 17) of all sizes to enter the splendid and most glorious mansions in the New Jerusalem, which he promised them, John xiv. And whereas thou wast not shown in thy dream, how the first casket was prepared, that being unnecessary, as thine own experience for the last few years would clearly come into thy mind, which, when compared with our history, brought to view in the xiv chapter of Rev. particularly 6-11 verses, would show thee how it was done. And the oneness of the angel or messenger in performing this first work, will help thee to understand, how the man (or messenger) which thou sawest enter the room will also be distinctly seen; since our great disappointment in Oct. 1844, operating under the divine guidance of the word and spirit, as far as can be seen through the gross darkness and infidelity that is becoming more and more manifest; through all of their instrumentalities, such as prayer, exhortation, visiting, comforting, writing, especially epistolary correspondence, and all other proper means to ascertain the whereabouts, and the number of the scattered sheep of the house of Israel: even the most lonely and most despised.

Wait patiently therefore and watch, remembering what God has taught in these last few years respecting the clear fulfillment of his word in our experience, and the perfect harmony we are now *made* to see in *place, manner* and *time*, for every point. As he had distinctly taught us, viz. "Which ye shall proclaim in their seasons." "A time for all things." "Every thing on his day." "Not one jot or tittle of the law to fail," even *the thoughts of God towards us to be perfectly considered in the latter* (or last) *days.*—Jer. xxiii: 20. As therefore it required the space of a few years to arrange and develope the first casket, so then here likewise must be *order* and *time* to cleanse, prepare, and properly arrange, the second casket, by the same kind of instruments.

And whereas thou didst cry to him to forbear for fear he would injure the precious jewels, and he replied fear not, I will take care of them; that is, those that are "keeping the commandments of God and the faith of Jesus," will not injure the jewels (their brethren) for they will act in harmonious concert, under the new commandments of their officiating great high priest and king.

Your cry to forbear, looks ominous of further resistance  and as for any of your assistance in collecting, cleansing and arranging the jewels of the Lord of hosts (the last casket,) it looks still more dubious, as it seems you kept your eyes closed (in a quiet state,) until the jewels were all arranged. This is the reason why you did not see the pains that the man (or messenger) took in arranging them.

This I fear, that you will not open your eyes to see this important work until the sealing time, and God speaks himself; but I cannot but still hope that your "shout for very joy," will be one of triumph and redemption.

Several nights before I saw your dream, I had finished writing your letter, I presented the subject of my work before the Lord again, for wisdom to direct me in all that I had, or may write for the benefit of his children, and the vindication of his word. And that I may do so, I asked for a dream, vision, or any way that was consistent with his will to instruct me. The next thing, as near as I can now recollect, was the following

Dream.

A great tumult behind me, with corresponding commotion in the heavens, so fully confirmed me that the Lord Jesus was coming, that I began to sing and rejoice; very soon the people began to assemble around me. They wanted to hear my opinion about the coming of the Lord. I felt no spirit of communication; my work seemed to be done, except to answer a few questions put to me by one or two out of a great number of backslidden adventists that seemed to be engaged in almost *any* thing but the work of God. This scene soon changed, and I was in meeting with a large assembly of worshippers. The speaker arose and pointed to a man that he said was under *conviction*; he seemed very anxious that I should see him. The congregation seemed to have a oneness with the speaker looking at him and myself. I looked, and although the man's head was resting on the railing of the seat, I perceived that it was an old neighbor of mine, who had lived and *died* a Universalist, several years ago. The preacher's theme, and whole labor, was, look! behold! this man is under *conviction*! I thought if they knew the man as well as I did, their wonder would soon cease. No other effect was produced, by this effort, other than to remind me of the extra exertions that had been made by the leading professed adventists since the spring of 1845, to prove that God was converting souls under their labors. Here the scene changed again, the house was cleared, and the seats laid away. The room now appeared very large, with a high stage at one end, on which I was standing with an instrument like a mallet in my hand, knocking off the top of a large box. A few spectators on one side, and a large fleshy man, the owner of the box, on the other, apparently very unwilling for me to open it. But it seemed a clear duty that I was fully authorized to examine all contraband goods, and therefore there was no resistance. As the top of the box flew off, this man eagerly seized two or three bottles apparently filled with water and hugged them close to him, silently waiting the result of the examination. The box was about one-third full of what appeared to be wooden feet and legs—it seemed as though they were painted idols. Among them was a very large glazed wide rimmed hat, with the hatters block fitted into it. I looked up to the man and exclaimed! what in the world did you smuggle this hat with a block of wood in it, in here for. The man still grasping the bottles, (I have thought emblematical of the water of life,) darted away to the east end of the room, and entered what appeared to me a closet door painted light blue, from which I could discover no light. Now, dear sir, as I have candidly, and prayerfully attempted to interpret your dream, will you write the interpretation of mine, and receive my love and earnest desire for your perfect reconciliation with God, and all his precious jewels in the last casket.

# Joseph Bates. Scriptural Observance Of The Sabbath.

The only safe rule, is according to the commandment; see Exo. xx: 8-11. This is the manner the disciples kept it; Luke xxiii: 56. The great God of heaven instituted the Sabbath, or day of rest, when he ended his six days work of creation, rested himself and sanctified the day, and thereby set the example for man. As there was but one man then, it is evident that it was not made for him alone, nor for any particular nation or people that should afterwards come—for he is said to be "no respecter of persons." Some think it was made for the Jews alone; but the commandment refers us to the creation, twenty-five hundred years before there was a Jew on earth. It also requires the stranger (the Gentile) to keep it, and God has promised to make him joyful in his house of prayer, by doing so; Isa. lvi: 6, 7. He has also given this day of rest to the beasts of burden, and makes man accountable for causing them to violate his day. They cannot speak for themselves; how important, therefore, that we should not, in any way, allow our beast to labor on that day. But, says the objector, surely there is no harm in using my horse to carry my family three or five miles to meeting on the Sabbath. The word says "obedience is better than sacrifice." If the meeting cannot be nearer home, and we cannot walk, why, then go before the Sabbath commences and stay until the day has ended. If a general meeting, and all cannot be accommodated, then it would be proper to have it some other day. God has plainly taught us how we shall keep this day: "We are not to do our pleasure on his holy day, but call the Sabbath a *delight*, the *holy* of the Lord, *honorable*, and shalt *honor him*, not doing our own *ways*, nor finding *our own pleasure*, nor *speaking our own words*, then thou shalt *delight* thyself in the Lord," and he will bless thee. See also what to us an unaccountable promise God made to his chosen people, if they would not carry any burdens in nor out of their houses, nor do any work on the Sabbath day: "The city of Jerusalem should stand forever."—Jer. xvii: 22-25; see also how Nehemiah enforced the sacredness of the day,—xiii: 15-21. Moses also, and many others; shewing clearly that God gave more directions about the fourth commandment, and greater promises, than for all others of his laws, and says "Verily, my Sabbaths ye shall keep that ye may know that I, the Lord, do sanctify you." And as I think that I have made it plain and positive from the scriptures alone, that the Sabbath was never changed nor abolished, then how simple, plain and safe to follow the example of our Father in heaven. Surely no living person can be condemned for this. Then let us keep the day as the bible teaches us that he did.

The Sabbath, God says, is a sign and covenant between him and the children of Israel *forever*; see Exo. xxxi: 16, 17; Ezek. xx: 12, 20. Read the curse that followed their violating it—xxii: 8, 25-28. Do you still say this is only for the

Jewish dispensation? read in Deut. vii: 9, the promise to them who keep his commandments to a *thousand* generations. Suppose a generation to be thirty years: then you have 24,000 years yet to come. But allow the scripture rule, *seventy years*, and then we have not reached that point by at least 64,000 years. Do you think his mercy will cease then, so many ages after immortality? It is not in the power of man to make a figure of this. Some other passages regard generation and generation, without limitation.

# Under The Gospel.

Christ, the Son of God, and his Disciples, kept the same Sabbath—(it is folly to speak of any other, the scriptures forbid it.) He was the Lord of the Sabbath, and he said it "was made for *man*."—Mark ii: 27, 28. For what man?—[See article, 2d Pillar.] He says he kept his Father's commandments. Paul says they are holy, just and good. John says, they are from the *beginning*, and points a company who are now keeping them. James tells us we are to keep the whole—surely the Sabbath is here; God himself, says it is.—Exo. xvi: 27, 28, and xx: 8-11.

Jesus, then, is our example. Surely we shall not err if we follow him. Respecting working, cooking, making fires, &c. &c., please see my reply to Barnabas. Jesus always preached on the Sabbath, and healed, and wrought miracles, and blessed his honest followers. And I know for one that he blesses them still, who worship on that day; see Mark vi: 2, "And when the Sabbath day was come, he began to teach in their synagogues," "as his custom was." Luke iv: 16, 31, he asked "if it was lawful to do well on the Sabbath days?" If we can do good in like manner, we shall be perfectly safe; if better, try it. Just read in the following passages, how and what he did. His being judged by primitive and modern professors, is no rule for us, "What is that to thee, follow thou me."—Matt. xii: 1-15. He shows that his disciples were "guiltless for eating," 7th v. They were soon into their meeting; see, he's at work immediately, 13th v.; see Luke xiii: 11-17, healing the woman; how withering his reply to his enemies, 14th v. I would that his adversaries were as much ashamed now; 17th v. See xiv. chapter, 1-6, and 7-14; here he went in to eat bread on the Sabbath day; 1st v., here he cures the dropsy and teaches them how to treat the poor, &c. See also John v: 1-20, and vii: 21-24, he shows that all of this is not (servile work) but works of mercy and necessity. He even instructed his disciples, Jew and Gentile, respecting the sanctity of THE Sabbath, thirty-six years after his death, Matt. xxiv: 20. In chapter v, he shows that the keeping of the *law*, &c., will make us great in the kingdom of heaven, 17-19. Then in 38-48 verses, shows us that under the Gospel, we are to follow his teachings and that we are now about to make the change from the ministration of Moses to that of his own, in the Gospel. Do see how *John* puts it together, Rev. xii: 17; xiv: 12, explained to be the spirit of prophecy, in xix: 10. Now every law with respect to the keeping the commandments and of course the Sabbath, is embraced in the testimony of Jesus. The special messenger of the Lord to the Gentiles, to teach them the abolition of Moses's ministration in the law, observed the Sabbath in obedience to his master; see Acts xvii: 2: xiii: 42-44, preaching to the Gentiles, 42 v.; xvi: 13, by the water side; xviii: 4, every Sabbath; 11 v. seventy-eight in succession. Luke records these, many years after the law of Moses was abolished. John had his vision on the Lord's day. Jesus never claimed any day for his, but the seventh-day Sabbath, Mark ii: 28; neither did his Father, Exo. xx: 10. Therefore, in following the authority and example of God, Jesus Christ, and the holy Apostles, we shall meet our glorious king with clear consciences. We never need to fear of keeping the holy and sanctified Sabbath day too strict. We cannot keep it holy, nor acceptable, if we employ *men* or *beasts* to labor for us on that day, neither printers, postmasters, nor carriers. The day is not ours, it is the Lord's: follow the Scripture rule, and the Sabbath will be a delight to us, and God will sanctify and save.

# The Beginning Of The Sabbath.

Here, also, we cannot be too particular; God claims every moment of his day. Out of one hundred and sixty-eight hours in the week he claims twenty-four, and gives man the balance, one hundred and forty-four, to do his servile work. According to the record of Moses, in Gen. i: 2, God commenced the motion of this Planet from a chaotic state of darkness, and sent it flying round the sun at the rate of about fifty-eight thousand miles per hour. He "divided the light from the darkness, and God called the light day, and the darkness he called night, and the evening and the morning were the first day,"—4, 5. God "made the sun and the moon; the sun to rule the day, and the moon the night, to divide the light from darkness."

Jesus says "are there not twelve hours in the day?" Well, then, there must be twelve hours in the night, to make a twenty-four hour day, and it must be equally divided, for us to keep the weeks correct. For example—say now the first of Jan., the inhabitants of the north pole have no sun, while those at the south have the sun all the twenty-four hours; now as we approximate to the centre or middle of the globe from the south pole, we shorten the days, but from the north we shorten the nights; when arrived at the centre, or under the sun, (the great time piece for the inhabitants of all the earth, Deut. iv: 19,) we find the days and nights are equal. At the beginning of the sacred year, for the passover, the sun rises at 6 A. M. and sets at 5 P. M., and there is not an inhabitant on any part of this globe that can regulate the time for day, or night without admitting the polar distance into his calculation, which is 90° from the centre. This at once shows that all the way we can calculate time is by calculating from the centre of the earth, and also bringing the sun there, if his declination be north or south. Therefore by the same rule (and no other,) we regulate the weeks, and must of necessity begin the scripture day at 6 P. M., or else being in one place, we never have two Sabbaths begin at one time. Says the objector we might begin at sunset. If so, no two persons could keep the same time except they were directly north or south of each other. But can they keep the same time all over the globe if they begin at six P. M.? Yes, certainly. For example.—Jerusalem being about 90°, or fifty-four hundred geographical miles east of us, makes a difference of six hours; it is six P. M. with them when it is noon day with us; their Sabbath closes then, six hours before it does with us—but it is at six o'clock P. M. there. And so when the Sabbath closes here, although it is precisely the same hour of the day, viz. six P. M., and in like manner all round the globe. Hence the necessity of beginning the twenty-four hour day at sun set from the centre of the earth. We are told that we cannot keep time right, because men, who circumnavigate the globe, make a difference of twenty-four hours in time. Well, suppose men could girt the globe with their magnetic wires, so that half of the inhabitants of the United States could pass clear round ten times a day, what odds would that make to the motion of the globe. This looks like another snare of Satan. The change from old to new style, they say, if eleven days are taken from the calender then that certainly has changed the seventh day, but some how or other it does not affect the first day, Sunday. How is it done? say some two hundred members in the British Parliament on Thursday, at six P. M. the first day of Jan. pass a unanimous vote by uplifted hands that we drop eleven days from the calendar. Now all the change here, is, it is now a few minutes past six P. M. on the same Thursday night called the eleventh of Jan. God never stopped the earth's motion one moment to listen to them. This certainly did not effect the day of the week, any more than the sun's standing still a whole day, that being true also, at 4 P. M., did not prevent them from counting Friday when it came. If he stood still for twenty-four hours, then no time would be lost to us, for Friday could not come until six, P. M., two hours after he started again. If it had been less than twenty-four hours then must it be regulated. The shadow going back ten degrees or forty minutes on the dial of Ahas, ("not ten hours,") was another miracle, but it remains to be proved that the *sun* went back. If any thing could possibly affect the time before the christian era, Jesus certainly had the correct *time, the Sabbath* before he was crucified. Astronomers can find no change since. If the christian era was four years out of date, it does not follow that the day of the week has changed since God instituted the Sabbath in Paradise. Gen. first chapter teaches when the sun is up it is day or morning; when he is down it is night, or evening. God reckoned the first six days from evening to morning; but further on, in the history of the world, he says "from even to even shall you celebrate your Sabbath," or rest. This proves that every day in the week began at evening; so it must continue while we have day and night. Surely God has done all things well, but man has sought out many inventions. God help the little flock to follow the truth, and "Remember the Sabbath day and keep it holy." Amen.

# The Last Experiment On Definite Time; The Prolonging Of The Days *All* Failed.

In 1843, the Herald and Midnight Cry for many months stated that all the signs preparatory to the second coming of Christ, were in the past. Soon after the passing of the *time* in 1844, they changed their minds and told us that we had but "just entered upon the ground of disputed chronology and that we should be justified in looking with more and more confidence to the extreme boundary of 1847, the extreme point of time in *dispute*."—See Advent Harbinger, Sept. 28th, 1847. On the strength of this, A. Hale came out with his definite time—LAST EXPERIMENT.

Well, we have now come to Jan. 1848, and all has failed. What is the matter? Answer—the disputed time was properly named; there is no truth in it. It is all a perfect failure; hence all their boasting ends with it. We say the cry at midnight, was right, and the appointed time did end in the fall of 1844, as shown in the *Way Marks*. We will now try some further proof, and still farther that their confessions and reorganization have fairly led them into the Laodocean state of the Church. They say that Christ may come any time; this is the teaching of all three of the Editors, and some of them talk loudly about the ending of the 2300 days, at that point of time. How vain to assert that the 2300 days will end here, the first of January. It is well known that the spring, or fall is the only place ever fixed for their ending.

Those who believe that Christ was crucified any where but in the middle of the week are teaching, as H. H. Gross, that his advent will be in the spring. Those who still believe in the types, and that Christ was crucified in the midst or half of the week can see no place for the ending of the 2300 days or the advent of Jesus, but in the seventh month. Neither can the 6000 years end any where but in the seventh month; the proof is clear in Gen. i: 11, 12, and 29, that the seed and fruit was ripe for the harvest when God finished his six days; proof, Adam and Eve partook of it. It is also perfectly clear that God changed the beginning of the year from thence to the first month, to commence the feasts of the Lord and the types to which we have, and still may, refer; see Exo. xii: 2; xiii: 3, 4; xxxiv: 18; Deut. xvi: 1. This was the beginning of months and the beginning of the year, the passover month.

Now we say here, according to the scriptures, Christ was crucified on the 14th day of Abib, or April, in the midst (or middle) of the week, meaning the last week of the seventy. This is just 486-½ years; then the balance *eighteen hundred and thirteen and a half* years more, would just make the 2300 days, or years. Now carry the half year from the Passover to the fall of the seventh month, then you will have just 1813 full years to come. Then, of course, every full year unto the last, must end here; and it is not in the power of man to make them end any where else, but in the seventh month. Neither is it in the power of any adventist, who says he believes in the speedy coming of Christ, to show any thing about their ending, since Oct. 1844, because we never have, and it is not likely we ever shall know of any other place or point, for their ending. If the beating of the air, three years, has proved a failure, and made the subject gross darkness, what can be expected from a farther experiment. If any one disputes this point, he will confer a great favor by showing where they do end.

There is *one* more point; that is, God's people are now in their trial foretold by prophets and apostles; and in their every day experience. If they deny this, then they cannot look for Jesus, because that trial must take place here in *time*; and according to the type, it must be while Jesus our great high priest is cleansing the sanctuary—for by turning to Lev. xxiii: 27-32 verses, we see the type of affliction was always on the tenth day of the seventh month, in the day of atonement, and it continued all the time that the high priest was in the most holy place, cleansing the sanctuary. The reason for this is obvious; if we turn to Lev. xvi: 15—"And he shall make an atonement for the holy place *because* of the *uncleanness* of the *children* of *Israel*, and *because* of *their transgressions in all their sins*," &c.; see also 29-34 verses, particularly the 30th verse. Then the true meaning of the cleansing of the sanctuary is, Christ our high priest in the sanctuary which the Lord pitched and not man; Heb. xiii: 2, that is, the new Jerusalem in the heavens, making atonement, or blotting out the sins of his true waiting people; and while he is doing this, they are in their trial. "Here is the patience of the Saints," as it was in the type referred to, with this difference—their day and trial and atonement was "from even to even," just twenty-four hours, whereas ours is to be from the tenth "day of the seventh month, until God roars out of Zion and utters his voice from Jerusalem," then Jerusalem will be *holy*, the atonement will be finished.—Joel iii: 16, 17— God's people be cleansed, sealed, and the captivity of Zion turned. This will be the shaking of the Heavens and the earth, the sea and all nations. Matt. xxiv: 29; Amos i: 2; Hagg. ii: 6-7; Jer. xxv: 30, 31; Heb. xii: 26; Eze. xiii: 25, 28. According to the signs given by Jesus, the next after this will be the sign of the son of man in heaven; "And then the son of man."—Matt. xxiv: 30. But as the world is to be taken by surprise, "crying peace and safety," they will not long be troubled with the shaking of the heavens and earth, it will pass from the mind, most likely, as has the *cry at mid-night*, so that after this, Christ will "come as a thief." But I do not design now to take up the argument, but merely refer to these points to show our position. For further reference, see Way Marks. I now propose to show the certain failure and confusion of all those Adventists who have denied the past, and the ending of the 2300 days. As I have already shown, they have prolonged, or, as in Prov. x: 27, "added to the days." The 2300 days, all the time from where they ended, Oct. 1844, to the extreme end of 1847, which would be three and a half years. Hosea calls this removing the bounds; well, we see they have finally moved them 1260 days. But God calls to Ezekiel and says: "What is that proverb that ye have in the land of Israel, saying the days are prolonged, and every vision faileth. *Tell them therefore*, thus saith the Lord God, I will make this proverb to cease, and they shall no more use it as a proverb in Israel, but say unto them the days are at hand and the effect of every vision, for there shall be no more any vain vision, nor faltering devination within the house of Israel; For I am the Lord, I will speak, and the word that I shall speak shall come to pass; It shall be no more prolonged, for in your days, O rebellious house, I will say the word, and will perform it, saith the Lord God" xii: 22-25. Three things here we notice; first, that the effect of every vision is to fail with the rebellious house of Israel. This, then, most certainly includes the *effect* of Daniel's vision on the second advent believers, it is the *effect* of *every vision*. The effect of John's vision fails with this. Now we actually know that the *effect* of Daniel's vision since 1842, has caused the whole world to tremble. We have no account in history that any vision, or all the visions of the prophets together, ever *began*, as it were, to have such an EFFECT as was produced down to Oct. 1844. *From that time the effect began to cease.* Second, here at the end of the prolonging of the days then, of this vision, God is to speak. It is well known that he never has spoken to the world since these prophets were born; therefore this is in the future, and right here at this point of time, and after this *effect*, and before the coming of Jesus. Third, then these days spoken of here are no other than the days of Daniel's vision, to measure time, for Ezekiel's vision nor any other vision given to the prophets, have chronological time to mark their fulfillment, save Daniel's and John's. Respecting the rebellious house of Israel, the prophets plainly and emphatically describe them to be in these last days, according to the texts above. The 27th and 28th verses of this xii chapter of Ezekiel, is more emphatic still: "They of the house of Israel (same rebellious house,) say the vision that he seeth is for many days to come, (yes, it is already advocated that  it is thirty years, in the future,) he prophesieth of the times that are far off." God says "there shall none of my words be prolonged *any more*, but the word which I have *spoken* shall be done saith the Lord God." Here, then, if we will believe God, no man after the prolonging of the days shall do it any more; that is, after the effect of the vision. What is the sign? Answer—God says, *He will* SPEAK. This, then, will end *all* the controversy. Now our history fully proves that the prolonging of the 2300 days with the effect of the vision, is claimed, to the end of the Jewish year of 1847, this spring. Now mark this! The rebellious house continue to say that these days, say Daniel's 2300, will not end until the coming of Christ, and he may come any time. I think I have proved conclusively that the 2300 days cannot end any where but in the seventh month; and the above scriptures and our history do clearly show that they have ended, and the time has been prolonged to the end of 1847. Now the seventh month 1847, is past, and this was the last point in their land marks, where the types, or seventy weeks shows they could end. It is impossible for any man to show their ending in the coming spring; and they have by their own showing forever shut themselves out for saying it will be in the fall of 1848, because this spring is the very extreme point to which the days are, or can be, prolonged. Here then, I say, according to the heading of this article, their last experiment fails, and fails them forever; they have no point to guide them to now, it is all gross darkness. Now if this is what the Bible Advocate calls "following the word of God and sound reason," I am glad that the shut door and Sabbath believers, are on the other side of the gulf, with "light in all of their dwellings."

Now let Zachariah, the prophet, finish this subject. In his peculiar view of the wonderful things to take place in the last days from the tenth to the fourteenth chapter inclusive, he says, "And it shall come to pass that in all the land, saith the Lord, two parts therein shall be cut off and die, but the third shall be left therein, and I will bring the third part through the fire and will refine them as silver is refined, and will try them as gold is tried; *they shall* call on my name and I will hear them, I WILL SAY IT IS MY PEOPLE; and THEY *shall say* THE LORD IS MY GOD."—xiii: 8, 9. Here then, is clearly pointed out the believers in the coming of Christ; a cry at mid-night shows first, but two parts; but before Christ comes Zachariah shows three parts. Now for the development of the history. The first is already described, by prolonging the days and denying the past. The three papers Advent Herald, Advent Harbinger and Bible Advocate, are still advocating their views, and as I have shown, *cut* themselves off. Second, class or part, are the spiritualizers; a large majority of which have joined the Shakers, whose faith is, that Christ came the second time in Ann Lee, more than seventy years ago, thus forever *cutting* themselves off from even looking for his personal appearing; John calls them anti-christ—thus, "Little children it is the last time, and as ye have heard that anti-christ *shall come*, even now are there many anti-christs (i. e. don't believe in any Christ—he is God, and God is love, &c.) whereby we know it is the last time: They went out from us, but they were not of us; for if they had been of us, they would no doubt have continued with us; but they went out that *they* be made *manifest* that they were not all of us. Who is a liar but he that denieth that Jesus is the Christ? *He is anti-christ* that denieth the Father and Son."—1st John ii: 18-22 verses. John classes all such with *liars*, and they are barred from the kingdom of heaven. In the 19th verse he says, "they were not ALL of us." This I think shows that some would see their error and repent. John here embraces *all* such believers from his day to the last. Here, then it is clearly manifest that this second part have cut themselves off! The third part are now in the fire (or fiery trial.); they are to be *refined* as silver, and *tried* as gold; they shall call on God, and they will be his people. They have nothing to boast of, they have got to overcome "by their perseverance."—[*Camp. trans.* of Luke xxi: 19.] Jesus also distinguishes them from the other parts: "They have a little strength (nothing to boast of,) and hast kept my word and hast not *denied my name.*" Which one? New name—King of Kings and Lord of Lords.—Rev. iii: 8, 12. The first and second classes have denied his name. The first say he is the Mediator, and therefore cannot have received his kingdom; the second class have dissolved his name into vapor. Ninth verse shows they have got to bow to his third part, because *they* have kept the word of his patience: Where is it shown that they do this? Answer—in Rev. xiv: 12th verse, "*Here is the patience of the Saints*; here are they that keep the commandments of God and the faith of Jesus." Yes! here are they who are denounced as "*door shutters*" and "great *sticklers* for the *seventh day Sabbath*, in and out of *almost every door* but the right one, following *any thing* but the *word* of God and *sound reason*!" triumphed at last. How amazing these things appear; not more so perhaps than to the prophets when looking down into our history and beholding this first class composed of the leading messengers and about all of the shepherds, after leading the whole flock out into the most dangerous part of their journey, desert, denounce, and betray them; and then go and form themselves into a confederacy and positively disregard the message which God pressed upon them, viz. "Comfort ye, comfort ye my people, saith your God," &c. I rejoice in my soul and praise the *living* God, who is seated upon this Great White Throne in the height of his Sanctuary in the heaven of heavens, that I am still numbered in this third part. Call me what you please, my feet are planted on the *Rock*. I had rather suffer affliction with the Outcasts, than enjoy the pleasures of sin with all other people. Praise the Lord! if faithful, we shall soon enter the everlasting kingdom. Amen.

# Christ's Second Coming To Gather His People.

According to the Scriptures, God will deliver his people out of the time of trouble that is now flying from the coasts of the earth, and to all appearances forming a junction in this retributive land of blood and slavery; by his VOICE *from heaven,* when he has sealed them, and Christ has made the atonement and fitted the mansions in the New Jerusalem, then they will be his chosen ones to execute the "judgment written." After this, in the order of events, the Lord Jesus "will descend from heaven with a shout, with the voice of the archangel, and with the trump of God," &c. When God speaks from Jerusalem, then, I believe the "wise will understand" how long it will be before Jesus comes. "The times and seasons are with the Father." I believe that the Scriptures most clearly teach Christ's second coming at the feast of Tabernacles, and no where else; and that our history, in the fulfillment of prophecy, has been imperceptibly tending us there. Here is the chain in the types: "THREE *times a year shall* ALL *thy males appear before the Lord thy God.*" These three feasts are typical of three of the most important events since the birth of our Lord Jesus Christ, and every advent believer should have a clear understanding of them. 1st, The feast of the Passover; 2d, Feast of Weeks; 3d, Feast of Tabernacles.

*First feast* was the crucifixion of our Lord at the Passover, on the 14th day of the first month, at 3 o'clock P. M.; the very day and hour the lamb was offered in the type for sixteen hundred and seventy years.

*Second feast*—the day of Pentecost, 1670 years from the time that the commandments were uttered by the voice of God, in the morning.—Exo. xix: 16; see Acts ii: 15, undoubtedly at the same hour. Now as these two feasts are perfectly fulfilled, we have nothing further to do with them here; only to say, that God never taught any other way to find the fulfillment of these two most important events, than by their typical observance.

*Third feast*—on the 15th of the seventh month; the feast of the Tabernacles. This undoubtedly represents the gathering of all Israel at the coming of Christ; the ingathering of the harvest; the end of the 6000 years: the end of the world. I see no other point of time for Christ to come than at the feast; see Deut. xvi: 1-16: Lev. xxiii; Num. xxviii, and xxix. It cannot be possible that God has been so exact in the fulfillment of the first two, to the very hour of the day, and then left the other without *order or time*! No, no! Here is the gathering of all Israel; see Lev. xxiii: 39-44. Now, this being true, all of the other events which precede this in this chapter, must, to harmonize with the types, be fulfilled first. Now there are three types in this feast; their harmony and order are as follows: First,—24th verse is the memorial of trumpets. This is the type of the sounding of the seventh trumpet; there is nothing else for an anti-type—try and see. Than it is fulfilled, by Rev. x: 7—"In the days of the voice of the seventh angel, when he shall begin to sound, the Mystery of God should be finished." &c. This then, we have shown, sounded on the first day of the seventh month, 1844. Here the virgins were divided, and the wise ones got ready for the coming of the Bridegroom to the marriage. See *Way Marks*, 35 to 37th pages.

*Second type*—27th verse—"Also on the 10th day of the seventh month, there shall be a day of atonement,—ye shall afflict your souls, for whatsoever soul it be that shall not be afflicted in that same day, he shall be cut off from among his people." This, of course, was artificial; but it was a type to represent the tried state which the virgins in the parable entered into on the tenth day of this seventh month, 1844, when they see their Lord did not come. Here is where the atonement commenced with the affliction, and as they ended together in the type, so we believe they will in the anti-type, when God speaks from Zion.—Joel iii: 16, 17; see *Way Marks*, pp. 58, 59. Now it is certainly evident that God's people are in this very state. This, then, according to the type, proves the Bridegroom as High Priest, officiating in the Sanctuary, making the atonement for this same people.

*The third type* in order, and the last in this feast, is the feast of Tabernacles, 34-39-44th verses. This is yet to come—the true point of our deliverance. What a harmonious perfect chain is here. Just see first day of seventh month, 1844; the seventh trumpet sounds, and the Mystery of God is finished; third wo come; virgins divide; on the tenth day of the same month, Bridegroom comes to the wedding; marriage takes place; door shut; Jubilee trumpet sounds to prepare for the Jubilee and Supper in the kingdom of heaven; cleansing of the Sanctuary commenced; the virgins on their trial; the appointed time, the 2300 days ended, and a cry at midnight, with all its messages. If the seventh trumpet has began to sound, then the rest have followed. If the saints are now in their trial, then, the seventh trumpet must have sounded first, or confusion would follow in the types. Destroy one link, and the chain is broke. Take it in all its parts, it is perfect, harmonious, and complete. Here, too, I understand, ends all the days of Daniel. The chart is perfect, and has answered its end. The world here also received their last warning. The Gospel age ends; the message is, "comfort ye, comfort ye *my* people." If this was not all done before Christ should come, the scriptures would be broken. It is perfect nonsense to talk of having these things done at his coming, or after he comes. Tell me, if you can, how Christ can atone for his people in the Holiest of Holies, at his coming? And then tell me where the saints are to be on their trial, if they wait his coming first? Tell me, if you can, where you will place the third wo, which brings in the time of trouble, of which the saints are to be delivered? Tell me, if you can, how, and for what purpose the seventh messenger will begin to sound his trumpet, while Jesus is sounding the trump of God, and shouting for his saints to leave the earth in a moment? And as the seventh messenger is some of the living saints, tell me, if you can, how they will have time even to turn and say the Mystery of God is finished? Tell me, if you can, why God is going to have every thing in confusion at that day, when he has always had perfect order in heaven and earth, ever since the creation? Two things to be kept in remembrance:

FIRST—The 11th chapter of Revelations does not teach the coming of Christ in the spring, nor at any other point.

SECOND—The ingathering of *all* Israel *after the Voice of God* is most clearly taught to be at the feast of Tabernacles, the last type in the feast, yet unfulfilled. All the others that have been, and are *now* fulfilling in these feasts of the Lord, have been tested to the day, and even to the hour of the day.

# A Correction.

I perceive that I have made a mis-statement, on page 56, 13th line; also page 59, sixth line from the top, in calling the 15th day of the first month, a holy convocation day, instead of the 14th, which always commenced at the beginning of the 14th day and ended where the 21st began.—Exo. xii: 18. The wafe sheaf also, was to be waved on Sunday morning, the morrow after the Lord's Sabbath—Lev. xxiii: 3, 11—all which makes the resurrection on the third day as clear as light—two nights and three days.

# Seventh & Fourteenth Of Revelations.

A further History of the Second Advent Doctrine, from its commencement to the treading of the Wine Press, &c.

With The One Hundred And Forty-Four Thousand Living Saints, Which Are To Be Gathered At The Second Coming Of Jesus, From Every Nation, Kindred, Tongue, And People; Especially Those That Are Now Occupying The Position Referred To In The Twelfth And Thirteenth Verses Of The Fourteenth Chapter.

Second Advent History.

In the fourteenth chapter of Revelations, John gives a most graphic delineation of the Second Advent movement, from its rise in about 1840, to a glorious state of immortality. He begins to describe from this never-to-be-over-looked, wonderful picture of the last days, forming, and changing in quick succession, under the deep impressions made on the heart, by the heavenly flying messengers, saying with loud voices—the hour of his judgment is come; and reminds one in some of its features, in the changing of positions, of that last dreadful conflict of nations, on the plains of Waterloo, which decided the fate of Europe. So here, in this last great conflict of contending armies, John, in his vision, hears a glorious voice, [see i: 15 and xix: 6.] and harpers harping with their harps. His eye is turned to the point from whence came the heavenly music, and he beholds a glorified company, with their INVINCIBLE Commander, standing away up on the Mount Zion, that had followed him through his fiery trying conflict, and he had brought them off victorious, and clothed them with immortality and everlasting life; and the Father had stamped "his name in their foreheads," and they numbered 144,000, redeemed from the earth; all the living saints that are saved out of the mighty host of nations. Now read the first five verses of this chapter and methinks you will agree with me, that John is here describing the character of the 144,000 as he had seen them sealed, as stated in the seventh chapter; where he closes their history with the 8th verse, to describe the dead saints, and seven angels with their trumpets, and the effect produced by them, from the 7th chapter, 9th verse to the 12th chapter. Then in the 12th and 13th chapters, the dragon, the beast and his image, &c., &c. And then he takes up the history of this same 144,000, from where he had seen them sealed in the 7th chapter, 4-8 verses; and begins by describing them sealed and redeemed from the earth, in company with the Lamb—the Lord Jesus. From the 6th to the 14th verse, he gives the outline of what they had been passing through, and the mighty host with whom they had been engaged. It will here be remembered that this message, or proclamation of "the hour of his judgment," has gone to every nation and tongue, and people; therefore as Jesus has stated that his elect are to be gathered from the four winds, or from one end of heaven to the other, then his 144,000 will be composed of all nations, particularly the poor ignorant, but honest hearted Slaves of this doomed country. But more especially those described in the 12th verse, walking out in their faith of all the living *present truth.*

An objection may arise with some; still, supposing that the 144,000, because they are named after the tribes of Jacob in the 7th chapter, they cannot mean the Israel of these last days. Micah, speaking of Jesus, says, "He is *to be* the ruler in Israel."—v: 1-2. Gabriel said he would "reign over the house of Jacob *forever.*"—Luke i: 33. Paul says "they are not *all* Israel that are of Israel;" "If ye be Christ's then are ye Abraham's seed and heirs according to the promise." When John was afterwards giving a description of the holy city, he even saw the names of the twelve tribes of the children of Israel inscribed on the twelve gates. This agrees with the description in the 7th chapter, and makes a perfect harmony when we understand that this vision was sixty years after the introduction of the gospel, when the church was the whole Israel of God. The other view would give the literal seed of Jacob full possession of the city; the gates being theirs by the titles on them. This would make a division wall there, and God would be a respecter of persons. The gentiles could have no claim there; thus their joint heirship with Christ would fail and so would this Revelation; for John was directed to "show (us) things which would shortly come to pass."—i: 1; and to "write the things which thou *hast seen,* and the things which are, and the things which *shall be hereafter*" in the churches, in the future.—xxii: 16. So we see this vision was all of the present and future; besides the tribes of *literal* Israel had before this been rejected and were to "be trodden down until the times of the gentiles were fulfilled."

To make the 14th chapter more plain, in respect to the 144,000, we will try to give an exposition of the 7th. "And after these things, I saw four Angels standing on the four corners of the earth, holding the four winds of the earth, that the wind should not blow on the *earth,* nor on the *sea,* nor on any *tree.* And I saw another angel ascending from the east having the seal of the living God; and he cried with a loud voice to the four angels to whom it was given to hurt the *earth,* and the *sea;* saying hurt not the *earth,* neither the *sea,* nor the *trees* till we have sealed the servants of our God in their foreheads."—1-3. I believe the general view of these four angels being the four leading governments [see 9th chapter 14, 15 verses,] is correct with the exceptions of Prussia or Rome, because neither of those nations have any maritime force on the sea. Great Britain, France, Russia, and the United States of North America, possess this power over all seas, and the most part of Christendom.

Our not being a party in the great christian alliance at the downfall of Napoleon Bonaparte, in 1815, neither in 1840, at the fall of the Ottoman Empire, will not, I think, effect this point; but being one of these four messengers, will make it clear, at least so far as relates to the flying messengers and their work, and our power on the sea. Who does this sealing angel ascending from the east represent? Answer—I think some of the very same flying messengers brought to view in xiv: 6, 7, and x and xviii chapters. If messengers in the form, and fashion of men, symbolically represented as flying through the midst of heaven, preaching the gospel to men, and "being clothed with clouds," rainbows and pillars of fire, lighting up the earth with their glory; standing upon the sea, and land, crying as when a lion roareth, that time should be no longer; are called angels, I see not, nor know of any other exposition of this second verse. If it is contended that an invisible angel is here described, then, according to the 9th chapter, 4th verse, it was done in like manner to individuals in the thirteenth century.

ASCENDING from the east, or sun's rising. I think this does not mean *rise up* out of, &c., as in chapter 13th, or *ascending* in a similar manner, as in chapter xvii: 8, but rather the following, for instance: these northern and middle States, and the Canadas, are now and have been the location of almost all the flying messengers, and the burden of their messages, as represented in the 14th chapter. William Miller began to proclaim the message from the west, (Low Hampton.) And now to reverse it, the sealing messenger is seen ascending from the eastern, the Atlantic States, bounded by the broad ocean, of nearly three thousand miles, which, when looking to the east, as John did at sun rising, would give the appearance of the sun's rising out of the water but a few miles off. Owing to the round surface of our globe, every 15°, or nine hundred miles that we sail from hence to the east, the sun appears *ascending* from his ocean bed one hour earlier in the morning. This is familiar to the mariner; as also when they discover another ship, they cry, "sail ho!" Why? Because the top of her sails are only seen, but as they approach each other, *ascending* up, as it were, out of the ocean bed, the lower sails, and then the hull, and soon after the men are distinctly seen upon her decks. If we look farther east for this sealing angel or messenger, even to Great Britain, or still onward to the northern coast of China, we shall find none that have been so much engaged in the work of God as those above described. But if it is still insisted upon, that this sealing angel is invisible, then we shall fail to know when we are sealed. But I think that it is a work to be done here, and the saints will understand when they are sealed or marked as readily as they did when they were rejoicing because they had got the victory over the beast and his image, on the sea of glass (or more sure word of prophecy.) Rev. xv: 2. This was their sectarian profession that bound them in Babylon; and now their second advent profession, as in Rev. xiv: 12, if adhered to, will bind them to Jesus and seal, or mark, them for the city; see xxii: 14. Ezekiel had a prefiguration of this, in his vision of the man clothed in linen with a writer's inkhorn by his side, passing through the city, marking God groaning, sorrowing children, (ix: 2, 4, 11,) preparatory to the awful slaughter that was immediately to follow; with the strict charge not to touch them that had the mark (or seal) in their foreheads;—just as it will be in the last days, when the 144,000, all of the *living* children, are sealed with the seal of the *living* God in their foreheads, having been marked or sealed in a similar manner, and by the remnant of the messengers that four years ago were writing, lecturing and exhorting the people of God to get clear of the mark of the beast by coming out of Babylon, because she had fallen; developing their true profession, or christian character, even then, by the help of the marking iron, (the steel pen and stamping type,) with the ink from the writer's *ink horn*; with this difference, that this simultaneous sealing of the 144,000 will show such a clear development of christian character in their lives and shining foreheads (or faces,) that it will be clearly understood that Jesus has redeemed them from *all* iniquity, by purifying "unto himself a *peculiar people*, ZEALOUS OF GOOD WORKS." [These good works, methinks, will be something more than simply saying we believe the Lord is coming.] Yes, says Malachi, when by his prophetic spirit, he saw Jesus "making up his jewels," at this point of time, "*then* shall ye return and discern between the righteous and the wicked, between him that serveth God and him that serveth him not." "In the latter (or last) days ye shall consider it perfectly."—Jer. Then "he that is unjust, let him be so, and he that is righteous, let him be so still, and behold I come quickly, &c."—Rev. xxii: 11, 12.

This sealing process, then, I understand to be going on with the little flock, progressing in accordance with the last eight years' peculiar labor in their experience, and will be completed and approbated by God in the agonizing time of Daniel's and Jacob's trouble, and proclaimed to the world by God's roaring out of Zion, and uttering his voice from Jerusalem; then he will be the hope of his people; (see Joel iii.) then their atonement will be finished, the Sanctuary cleansed,—16th and 17th verses; "Zion's captivity turned;" "their mouths filled with laughter;" "the jewels made up," and the wise will understand the time of their coming deliverer.[2]

*The four Angels.*—How does the sealing angel, or messenger, ascending from the east, cry with a loud voice to these four angels or governments of messengers, to "hurt not the earth, neither the sea, nor the trees," &c. In the first place, I understand that symbolic prophecies have literal statements interspersed, which serve as a key for the rest: i. e. they have a mixed character; for instance, earth and sea here, literal; *trees*, symbolical; meaning those that are *marked*, or *sealed*; the professed people of God—followers of Jesus. See the clear proof under the sounding of the fifth trumpet by the

Turks, in ch. ix: 4th verse: "they were not to hurt any tree, but only those MEN which have *not* the *seal* of God *in their foreheads.*" This proves the trees to symbolize the followers of God; see also Hosea xiv: 8. Again, it is said that these four messengers were to "hold the wind from blowing on the *earth, sea,* or any *tree.*" By the *wind,* I understand as Paul teaches the Eph. iv: 14, "every wind of doctrine and cunning craftiness, and slight of men to deceive, and lead nations into carnage, war and bloodshed;" see also ii: 2, "being led by the Prince of the power of the *air,* working in men disobedience, according to the course of this world." After the last great battle of nations at Waterloo, in 1815, then these blood-thirsty, conquering crowned heads, formed themselves into what they called a christian alliance, showing that there was now peace with all the world; since which time they and our own government have been petitioned or prayed to by those who professed to be the followers of the Prince of Peace, to abolish the wicked practice with themselves, and thereby restrain all other nations. Now let us learn the difference between the trees, (professors or followers of the Prince of Peace,) and *servants of God* which are now to be sealed, viz. the 144,000. Thousands on thousands of these professors or trees since this work began, have died, and probably one hundred times that number have turned traitors, by deserting their leader and commander, while the great mass of advent believers, which stamped this truth upon them, (the nominal church) in Oct. 1844, have since that time, also turned into the enemy's ranks, leaving the remnant to finish up the work. The great majority of these professors were once under the right banner, but the winnowing fan of their great leader has left them with the chaff, so that the voice of the remaining messengers, some of whom were sending these petitions to the four governments, and their prayers to God to restrain these wicked practices, have become so feeble and disregarded by their former associates, that the Devil, seeing his time is short, is now hard at work marshalling his united forces throughout the world, for a mighty victory; and these four messengers are his principle dependence to "gather the whole world to the battle of that great day of God Almighty," but it will not become general until the 144,000 saints are sealed.

Here, then, I understand, that the professed followers of the Prince of Peace, (symbolized as trees,) have been crying with a loud voice by their petitions, which is the symbol for prayer, see xiv: 15, 18, and Matt. xxvii: 46, praying these four messengers that have power on all lands, and *all* seas, not to make any more war, either on the land or on the sea, nor with the professed people of the Prince of Peace, by disregarding their petitions. I know not in what other way these four nations could be prayed to as represented in the second verse. Now the 144,000 are sealed. Then John brings us to the resurrection. The 9th verse says, *after this,* (mark this point,) I beheld, and lo, a great multitude which no man could number of all nations and kindreds, and people and tongues stood before the throne, clothed in white, with palms in their hands, &c. These I understand are *all* the sleeping saints from Abel down to the very last one that falls asleep here. Their having palms in their hands, and robed in white, looks to me like the perfect uniformity there will be with *them*, and the 144,000 that have never died, that I believe will be redeemed right from, or at, the time for the feast of Tabernacles, and form a perfect phalanx, rending the air with their shouts while they are mounting up with wings as eagles to meet their glorified king and Lord; see xix: 14; Lev. xxiii: 39-44. Here, they will serve God day and night in his temple.—15th verse. Therefore all the work that is pointed out here in Revelations for the messengers, (called angels,) to perform, will all be accomplished here before Christ comes. Now we will turn again to the

## FOURTEENTH CHAPTER OF REV., FIRST TO FOURTEENTH VERSE.

"And I looked, and lo, a lamb stood on the Mount Zion, and with him an hundred forty and four thousand; having his Father's name written in their foreheads.—And I heard a voice from heaven as the voice of many waters." Please turn back now to the beginning of the subject 19th page, you will see it is the Father's name written in their foreheads—i. e., they are now sealed— got through with their patient waiting time, and are marked with the name of God; see iii: 10-12. In the 2d verse is the voice; this I understand is God speaking after the saints are sealed, or Christ and the saints; see i: 15, and xix: 6, as presented on the 96th page.

"And they sung as it were a new song before the throne—no man could sing that song but the hundred and forty and four thousand, which were redeemed from the earth." [Margin says, *bought*.] Now mark! these were bought from the earth, and they sung a song that no man could learn. This must have been one which they had learned in their united experience, something like the song of Moses on the banks of deliverance from the Egyptians. No other people could have sung the song because it was the song of their deliverance, for as I have stated these first five verses show this 144,000 in their immortal state, "redeemed from the earth," (not out of it.) "These are they which were not defiled with women." "The woman which thou sawest is the great city which reigneth over the kings of the earth."— xvii: 18, called Babylon, (the nominal churches). These, then, were the same ones that had come out of the churches; see 8-11 verses, and xv: 2 verse. If the other view is insisted upon, then *all* of this 144,000 must be men and the women would have no part in that number—no matter where they are said to come from—"*for they are virgins.*" Being clear of the harlot mother and her children; and of those in the parable of the ten virgins that went into the marriage of the Bridegroom makes them emphatically so. "*These are they which follow the lamb whithersoever he goeth.*" The above shows that they did follow him, and John shows that they do now in their glorified state; see xix chapter, 14th verse. *"These* WERE *redeemed from among men being the first fruits unto God and to the lamb."*—4th verse. Redeemed or bought from among men (not from among the dead) nor from out of the earth, but from "among men and from the earth." The first fruits cannot be until the harvest, and that cannot be until Jesus comes to reap it with his sharp sickle, see 14th and 15th verses; remember too, that the description John is here giving, is the 144,000 with Jesus, after he has reaped the harvest of the earth.

See how perfectly it harmonizes with the type of Jesus being the first fruits, to God, or handful of the *first* harvest of barley to represent his resurrection; since which time he has been laboring with his Father for this very harvest. To have the figure harmonize the fruit must come at the harvest time, not the seed time. This is the first fruits unto God and to the Lamb conjointly. The dead saints are no where that I know of represented as fruits, before the resurrection. This then is the harmonious view; but we will look at the view which the Bible Advocate and others, have shown, that the 144,000 shown here, were the saints that came out of their graves after the resurrection.— Matt. xxvii: 52, 53; and we are told that "Eph. iv: 8, is to the point." "When he ascended upon high he led captivity captive"—[Margin says, a *multitude of captives,*] but this marginal reading so much relied on for their proof by the mark thus (∥,) shows it to be the view of the bible translators. Now to get the clear view, turn to the 68th Ps. 18th verse, from where Paul quoted. Here the marginal reading marked thus [Heb.] shows it to be the original, the inspired word. Now let us read—"Thou hast led captivity captive—thou hast received gifts in *the man,* (in Jesus) yea, for the rebellious also." This changes the meaning, and would make this multitude of captives rebellious saints. Surely Jesus took no such present as this to his Father; therefore there will be no more necessity for straining the plain text in Cor. xv: 20, 23. This text is clear, emphatic, and repeated; which distinctly teaches Christ the first fruits of them that slept; *afterwards* they that are Christ's at his coming, when both the dead and living will be the first fruits to God and the lamb conjointly. To harmonize the type, the saints at Christ's second coming are the next or second fruits to God at the second or last harvest in the 7th month, the revolution, or ingathering of the year, the feast of Tabernacles. Another writer J. Porter, states, that Jesus took these saints that arose at Jerusalem right up to his Father, and then received his power, and returned the same day; and he might also have added, travelled with the two to Emmaus, seven and a half miles; and as others will have it, was back time enough to keep the whole day with his disciples, for the first Sabbath after his resurrection. If we really want the truth, God will give it to us, but not by rejecting other truths.

Now let us see whether the description of character given in these five verses of the 144,000, will apply to the saints that arose in Jerusalem at the resurrection. In the first place, these were never numbered. Second—The record is entirely silent about their being united in their trials and experience, to sing a peculiar song of their own. Third—These were not redeemed from among men, on the earth, but out from among the dead. Fourth,—They could not be the first fruit before the harvest, for Paul says, "Christ the first fruits, *afterwards* they that are Christ's at his coming," (second coming,) not them that were his at his going away at his first advent,—first harvest. That would be a clear perversion of the text; we must wait for the second harvest for the next fruit, 7th month. Fifth—To say that they were virgins, and not defiled with women, is only admitting what we know nothing about. Sixth— John saw the messenger that sealed, and says the number was 144,000; all this, was sixty years after what transpired at Jerusalem. This is out of the limits of his vision; and what will, and does forever, destroy this erroneous view, is, that the four winds are to be holden by the four Angel nations, until the whole number were sealed, and they have not let go yet; unless it can be proved that it was done 1800 years ago. That old Jerusalem was called a holy place; see Exo ix: 8; Acts vi: 13; also the testimony of Jesus, Matt. xxiv: 15. Lastly—If it is objected that these are the living saints to be redeemed at the second advent, then we fail to find them described in this vision, which would destroy the chain of wonders which he saw respecting the living and the dead, with the varied and changing scenes through which they were continually passing. Now, how simple, plain, and harmonious these verses appear when we apply them down at the end of all things, where they were seen in this vision, and where they most certainly belong. The 5th verse shows them without fault before the throne, clearly in their redeemed and immortal state. Here then is the true description of their characters. In the next seven verses from 6 to 13, John describes

THEIR LABORS IN THE MESSAGES.

"And I saw another angel fly in the midst of heaven, having the everlasting gospel to preach, unto them that dwell on the earth, and to every nation, and kindred, and tongue, and people, saying with a *loud voice*, fear God and give glory to him, for the hour of his judgment is come."

This is so plain that all who have been engaged and laboring in the Second Advent Doctrine must admit it to represent William Miller, and those of his faith, as the flying messengers preaching the advent of Jesus to their fellow men, since 1840. Invisible angels never yet preached the gospel to men; but as it has been here—man preaching to man,—then these angels represent our own neighbors, preaching, lecturing, and exhorting us with loud voices to listen to their message, for the judgment was at hand.

He says he "saw another angel." Where did he see the first one, then? Answer—In his description of the trumpets, viii: 13, thus he carries our minds back to the simple narration of the first description of these messengers and receivers out of which were sealed 144,000, in 7th chapter. This message has gone to every nation, kindred, tongue and people.

"And there followed another angel saying Babylon is fallen, is fallen," &c., 8th verse. This fallen city, we say, was the nominal churches, embracing all of the professed followers of the prince of peace; and they have fallen, because they rejected this first message at the hour of God's judgment, and shut it out of their worshipping assemblies, and out of their hearts—"they *made light of it.*"

And the third angel followed, saying with a loud voice, "If any man worship the beast and his image, and receive his mark in his forehead or in his hand, the same shall drink of the wine of the wrath of God, which is poured out without mixture," &c.—9th and 10th verses.

These two last described angels, which follow the first, are only a part of the flying messengers described in the 6th and 7th verses—for many of the first class opposed the second and third messengers, and some absolutely denounced them for saying Babylon, or the nominal churches had fallen, and for calling God's people to *come out* of them and leave them forever. In chapter xviii, 4th verse, John heard the same voice from the same people, called the third angel, telling them to come out from Babylon. In the xiv. chapter, he more particularly describes the condition of all those who *retain* or *receive* again the mark of the beast, or in any way connect themselves with these churches,—Jer. iii: 3; the plain English of which is, get clear of this mark, or profession, and *keep clear*, come out and stay out of this "habitation of Devils." For a further explanation of these texts, and definition of the locations of the heavens, &c., see *Way Marks.*

Any advent believer who undertakes to dispute this, and the two preceding angels' messages, with their clear fulfillment in advent history from 1840 to the fall of 1844, is, in my opinion, but a few steps removed from the gross darkness that surrounds the habitations of Babylon. I will venture again to reiterate the assertion, that since the days of the Apostles, God's people have never witnessed such a simultaneous and righteous movement, as they did during these three messages. I feel perfectly safe in saying that I fear no contradiction here, nor condemnation hereafter, for moving in perfect harmony, as we have done, during these three messages. Many are writing and preaching that these are, and will continue to be given, while the world stands. This mistake is as fatal as the rejection of the first, because in so doing they will not see any work which God has marked out for them, in this last work for man to fulfill and finish the history of this prophecy. We say, then, that these messages closed with the world, when they were condemned by them, at the end of a cry at midnight, in Oct. 1844. God then had other and more important work for his church to perform among themselves than they ever had before, and it is clearly marked out in the verses which follow these messages, and whoever fails here, fails to follow the Lamb whithersoever he goeth. Be assured, John has not broken the thread of this most interesting narrative here and left us in confusion, to call the testimony of *Jesus his commandments*; and our resting from this most laborious work in these messages, *the resurrection*. If our experience, for more than three years past, has not taught us that God is fulfilling his word, by having every thing in its place; one thing following another, then we have failed to profit by it. Let me entreat you, my brethren, to critically examine the next three verses: viz. "Here is the patience of the saints, here are they that keep the commandments of God, and the faith of Jesus."—12th verse. What is the faith of Jesus? Answer,—Chapter 12th, 17th verse says it is his "testimony;" chapter 19th, 10th verse, says his "testimony is the spirit of prophecy." "Teach all nations to observe all things whatsoever I have commanded you."—Matt. xxviii: 20. Now observe, the faith, or testimony of Jesus, embraces all his teachings. Now mark, this is what our opponents call the New Testament *commandments*, or *grace*, which they say embraces all the commandments that we are bound to believe or keep!

The text says that these people that are in their patience, their *trying time*, keep the commandments of God, besides the testimony of Jesus. Here then, we are absolutely directed, not only to the old testament but to the decalogue— Exo. xx: 1-17, and even before there was any decalogue in the form of a precept; see Exo. xvi: 27-30. This one text, in itself, positively overthrows all of their unscriptural teaching about their New Testament commandments, and clearly demonstrates the perpetuity of God's holy Sabbath, because the commandments of God are one thing, and the testimony of Jesus is another. These are the people, then, and the only ones too, who abide by the whole word of God, in the Old and New New Testament teaching, and they that deny the teachings of this text, deny the word of God, and trample down His Holy Sabbath.

In the three preceding verses, God's people are called away, and required, under penalty of their salvation, to continue disconnected from Babylon, the churches to which the great mass before this belonged. Now the very next thing after these messages, John declares that they are keeping the commandments of God; that is, they are keeping the seventh-day Sabbath. Where is the proof? says the objector. Here it is—when this same people were making their sacrifice, in 1843 and '44, expecting the Lord to come, they were walking out in all the commandments of God, as far as they were taught or knew them at that time; and we all fully believed then, and do now, that *all* the honest ones were in a saved state; and if called away then, as was brother Fitch and others, the same hope would follow them; but we know that they could not be honest, nor be saved, if they were knowingly living in violation of any of God's commandments; and yet we all positively know *now*, that with a very few exceptions, we were all living in open violation of the 4th commandment, which we were taught to do, (though not always designedly,) in the churches to which they belonged, and where they are still continued to be taught; and our staying with them, *we now see*, would not have altered, for they *fell* for rejecting the message that came before this, and therefore the subject of this 12th verse was not presented to them. Our keeping the first day of the week for the fourth commandment, never was, nor ever will be, fulfilling it, any more than keeping Friday for the Sabbath. John, who kept the right Sabbath, and was now describing our real labors and characters, could not have said that we kept the commandments, unless we were keeping the seventh-day Sabbath, according to God's direction and *his* practice. This, then, being the only commandment that ever had been objected to, from the days of the Apostles, by those who pretended to keep them, makes it clear that John could not have had any reference to either of the others, but the Sabbath only. Here then, for the first time, they were *right* in the keeping of God's commandments; and the history of God's confiding children since the messages of 1844, are fully demonstrating this point, which clearly proves this exposition to be unobjectionable and *perfect*. Another point is, that they could not keep the seventh-day Sabbath, until they were separated and undefiled by the woman, (see 4th verse,) hence the declaration that they were doing so after the message of the third angel had separated them from Babylon. John saw the dragon making war with this remnant, (xii: 17,) and the unclean spirits coming out of the mouth of the dragon (or devil,) have been, and are now, doing this work. The very object in sending forth this work, has been to expose these deceivers, who for the last five months more especially, have been bearing down upon this remnant in a paper war, with all the power they could wield. We do not, by any means, expect this is all of it, because we know that the devil will never yield, nor discharge the volunteer company which he is so judiciously marshalling out of the second advent ranks, until every device to destroy the remnant is resorted to, and they are seen emerging from the smoke and carnage of this unholy warfare, ascending to the gates of the holy city, under the waving banner of the commandments of God.—Rev. xx: 11-14.

The judgment hour cry, in 6th and 7th verses, was the only one that was designed to go to all the nations of the earth; and that of itself was sufficient to condemn a world of sinners and false professors that rejected it. Other tests were required, especially in this land, more than England and other lands, because the light of the church was, and still is, in these middle and northern states. Here also, is where this doctrine emanated from; hence the other messages to test and bring out the true. Then those who reject the messages are the false ones; but the unlettered slave and those who have been, as it were, enshrouded in moral darkness, and have been honestly following the Lamb whithersoever he goeth, as far as they knew, have not rejected this light as have the advent believers in this land; therefore they are not under the same condemnation.

"And I heard a voice from heaven saying unto me, write: Blessed are the dead which die in the Lord from henceforth; yea, saith the spirit, that they may rest from their *labors* and their works do follow them," 15th verse.

I understand this verse as still referring to the same messengers and their adherents, who had been laboring almost incessantly to convince their friends of the reality of the messages, in an especial manner, during a cry at midnight, where they closed with the world. If it was not true of them then as a body, then there is no history  since John had this vision, to show any thing like it; and it looks like making scripture, to attempt its application in the future, disconnected with the labor in the preceding verses. The inference is natural, and it is just like God's order every where, that these his honest believers, should rest from their labors with the world, to get their own minds cloudy and calmly fixed on the great event before them. Isaiah saw it; see xxvi: 20, 21, and xxv: 19. How can God's children be shut away in their chambers from the world, and then say at his coming we have *waited* for him, if they were not resting from their labors with the world, doing what he says, in his 40th chapter 1st verse. It is also in perfect harmony with the type.

Do stop here a little while, and turn to Lev. xxii: 27-32, and show, if you can, where the harmony, anti-type, or clear fulfillment of these verses are, if they are not found in Revelations xiv: 12th and 13th verses.

*First*—then, the type in Leviticus: Here the primitive established church annually, on the tenth day of the seventh month, had a twenty-four hour day of atonement, to cleanse them from their sins. During these twenty-four hours they were positively required by the statute or law to enter into a *Sabbath* of *rest* and *day* of *affliction*, or *trial*, and rest from all their *labor*, "from even to even," under penalty of being forever cut off from his people.—29th and 30th verses. There is one more peculiar trait in this type which demands our particular attention; that is, in every other Sabbath or holy convocation *they* were positively required to abstain from all *servile work*—but in the tenth day it is not specified; see also Num. xxix: 7. This shows the perfect order of God that when the church in the last days should enter upon the anti-type, as in Rev. xiv: 12, 13, that they would not be required to cease from *servile work*, (if necessary), because the atonement for them would require more than twenty-four hours, seeing that them were 144,000 from every nation, kindred, tongue, and people; whereas those represented by the type could all be assembled in a few hours. This is also in harmony with the fourth commandment for *laboring* the other six days for food and raiment, as long as we keep the Sabbath even to the gates of the city.—22: 14.

*Second*—the anti-type—Rev. xiv: 12, 13. After passing through the messages above described they are now out of the Sardis, (or nominal,) into the Philadelphia state of the church, and commenced their day of atonement since Oct. 1844, they also enter into the same kind of rest by keeping for the first time the right Sabbath of the Lord our God in their *patient waiting*, or *trying time*; resting from their *labors*, in these messages, from the world: having now done with them; waiting for their great high priest to finish the cleansing of the sanctuary, which blots out their sins, and purifies them to enter into the holy city. The reason of the anti-type in the atonement, being longer than the type (twenty-four hours) is obvious, because God will give his people sufficient time to accept or refuse the light presented to them after their labors with the world, to perfectly fulfill the type, by voluntarily entering into this Sabbath and resting from their *labors*.

Will this be objected to because it reads "Blessed are the dead that die in the Lord from henceforth;" and must mean such as die a natural death. Well, Paul says "prove all things," &c. Suppose then we say this verse was to have its fulfillment from A.D. 96, when John wrote it, henceforth from that time. Then the strong and clear inference would be, that Stephen and James, and all the rest of the disciples who had died before, would not be blessed— because the blessing here given, is from the time when given, henceforward. If we move the beginning of this time to Luther's day, as some will have it, then we cut off John and all the saints up to that time; and if we move it to Oct. 1844, then we cut off every saint that has died in the Lord before.

But to get clear of all this, we are told that this 13th verse evidently represents the saints at the resurrection. (See Bible Advocate, Sept. 23, 1847.) He refers, (as I have,) to the advent message in 6th and 7th verses, but avoids the second and third angels' messages, (8-11 verses) or leaves them and the 12th verse also, to be fulfilled in connection with the 13th verse, at the resurrection. Then to make his view clear to our understanding, we must read it something like this: Blessed are the dead which die in the Lord, from the time the advent message began, (say 1840,) until Babylon falls, and the statement is being made about what is recorded in the 12th verse "where is the patience of the saints," &c. Well, say then, that one hundred saints, or more, have actually departed this life, since that time commenced, and they will be blessed at the resurrection. The question then arises—If this must actually be fulfilled for these few, where is the blessing for John, who had this vision, and all the saints who have actually died since 1840? Is God partial? Shall we find this distinction in the 7th chapter, 9, 10, 15 and 17th verses, where the great multitude of all the departed saints are represented before the throne of God with white robes, and palms in their hands? No. Shall we find it in the 20th chapter? where he says, "Blessed and holy is he that hath part in the first resurrection;" where not only the departed saints, but the 144,000 living ones, are brought to view? No—nothing of the kind. This Revelation was concerning *"things present,* (A.D. 96,) and things to come." We see, then, if this 13th verse, as we are told, does represent the departed saints any where, or time, since A.D. 96, and will be fulfilled at the resurrection, it is yet incomprehensible. Is it not clear that it only has reference to all the righteous saints in these messages from Oct. 1844? How can it mean the literal dead? Is it not clear that the dead know not any thing; therefore the blessing would not effect them as this text teaches any more than to bless any other inanimate substance. The Blessing belongs always to the living. Just look at Jesus' sermon on the mount.—Matt. v: 3-11—"Blessed are ye when men shall revile you, and persecute you, and shall say all manner of evil against you falsely, for my sake" &c. &c. This is now being fulfilled to the letter; see also Rev. i: 3; xvi: 15; xix: 9; xxii: 7; v: 12, 13; Luke xxiv: 50, 51, "Blessed are they that hear the word of God and keep it."—*Jesus.* "Blessed are they that *do* his commandments," they shall be saved,—xxii: 14. Also, Isaiah lvi: 2, that keep the Sabbath; these two last are to the point, just what they are doing in our text, 12th and 13th verses of Rev. xiv. John is here certainly speaking of a *class*, or *company*, of living believers, and not the literal dead. *Rest* is opposite to *labor*. He shows that the seraphim and cherubim, (invisible angels,) *rest* not day, nor night, but are continually "saying Holy, Holy, Holy, Lord God Almighty."—also v: 11, 12. The sleeping saints at the resurrection have no rest, they serve God *day* and *night* in his temple—vii: 15. Then the *rest* spoken of here in the 13th verse is of the living; resting from their labors with the world. Once more, "Blessed are the dead that die in the Lord." Paul said the commandment so affected him that he *died*—Rom. vii: 9. He means that he died to sin. Again, he says, "I *die daily*,"—1st Cor. xv: 31; "In *deaths* oft"—2d Cor. xi: 23; "If ye be *dead* with Christ," &c.—"For ye are *dead* and your life is hid with Christ in God" &c.—Col. ii: 20; iii: 3, 4; also, see Rom. vi: 8, 11, *"Dead* indeed unto sin, but alive unto God through Jesus Christ our Lord." In all these, and much more, he uses these terms for himself and others that were actually alive in the church. But the general term used for such as were literally *dead*, by Jesus and the apostles, are asleep; *they sleep*; "Our friend Lazarus *sleepeth*." He spake of his death; the people did not understand; he explained by saying *"plainly* he is *dead*."—John xi: 11-14. Paul says, "they also which are fallen *asleep* in Christ"—1st Cor. xv: 18; "Some are fallen *asleep*."— 6th verse: "We shall not all *sleep*, but we shall be changed."—51st verse: see also 1st Thes. iv: 15, "Them also which *sleep* in Jesus" &c.; "Since the Fathers fell *asleep*"—2d Pet. iii: 4.

*History.*—We prove these, then, to be a part of the same class of the messengers and their adherents that came out of the churches. Thousands of living testimonies could be adduced to prove the multitudes who died in the camp meetings and conferences, about the time that the messengers were closing up their messages. Why, many were burdened with the cry, die to sin, and the world; and live unto God. And thousands passed through this death struggle. Yes, they were blessed by *dying in the Lord*. Those who deny and make light of this part of our experience, were but little acquainted with the work of God in the fall of 1844, and need to be instructed again. But those that died to sin, and the world then; cannot be in a saved state now, if returned to the world. To be safe, follow Paul's example, "*die daily.*"

Then, without destroying one single link of this harmonious chain of events, these saints will be in the right place to fulfill the next message in the 15th verse, "crying with a loud voice," (different from the preceding ones,) this I understand will be a combination of labor among the resting ones, to be united in the incessant prayer, or crying to God day and night in the time of Jacob and Daniel's trouble (Jer. xxx: 7; Dan. xii: 1,) for deliverance, and for Christ to come on the white cloud, as represented in 14th verse, with his sharp sickle and reap the harvest for all things will appear to be ripe on the earth; see Sam. vii: 8; Jer. xxii: 4, 5; Mark xv: 34, 37; Luke xviii: 1, 7. Here, I believe, is where the 144,000 living saints of all nations, are sealed; especially will it be manifest among the tried ones then, that have passed through these messages. Then the four angel governments will cease to restrain war and bloodshed; God will speak as in Joel iii: 16, 17: the Sanctuary will be cleansed; the sins of God's people blotted out—in other words, the atonement finished and their trials ended; their captivity turned. Two such ones will then put ten thousand to flight. Jesus comes out of the most holy place, changes his garments, puts on his kingly robes and stands up to reign over the nations, as in Dan. xii: 1; mounts his cloudy chariot with his sharp sickle to reap the harvest of the earth. Here the 144,000 are in a state of deliverance, ready for the next and last message in the 17th and 18th verses. This message looks like one united and incessant prevailing prayer, (differing from all the others, because of the everlasting union that these messages have at length accomplished with these sealed saints,) ascending to God, while these messengers who have now, as it seems, become reapers similar to those in xix: 14, 15, "and are to gather the vine of the earth and cast it into the great wine press of the wrath of God," (19. v.) "to execute upon *them* (the wicked) the judgment written; this honor have all the saints. Praise ye the Lord." Now return to the 7th chapter, 9-15 verses—"After this," (when? after the saints were numbered and sealed,) "I beheld, and lo, a great multitude which no man could number, of all nations, and kindreds, and people and tongues, stood before the throne, and before the Lamb, clothed with white robes, and palms in their hands. And they cried saying amen, blessing, and glory, and wisdom, and thanksgiving, and honor, and power, and might be unto our God forever and ever, Amen." The 144,000 will then stand on the Mount Zion.

"Fear not little flock, it is your Father's good pleasure to give you the kingdom."

## CHRIST NOT REPRESENTED AS AN ANGEL.

Christ is no where represented as an angel, in Rev. unless it can be proved that he is so, in the 8th ch. 3-5 vs. He tells us that the 7 stars in his right hand are the angels, or messengers; see i: 20. He is called "one *like* unto the *son* of *man.*" Read his description i: 13-18; xiv: 14; the same in Dan. vii: 13; x: 5, 6; xii: 6, 7. He is also called the Lamb 26 times; see v: 6, 8, 12, 13 vs.; vi: 1, 16; vii: 9, 10, 14, 17; xii: 11; xiii: 8, 11; xiv: 1-4; xv: 3; xvii: 14; xix: 7, 9; xxi: 9, 14, 22, 23, 27; xxii: 1, 3. This Lamb is the Lord of Lords, and king of kings; and they that are *with him* are *called* and *chosen*, and faithful; see xvii: 14; xix: 16. He is called the *word* of God, and "the armies" the "chosen and faithful" ones follow him; see xix: 13, 14. He is called the *first* and the *last* i: 8, 17; ii: 8; xxii: 13. And the one which *was*, and *is*, and *is to come*, i: 4, 8; iv: 8; xi: 17. He is the *true and faithful witness* i: 5; iii: 14. Also the root of David, the morning star, xxii: 16; ii: 28; also Mich. xii: 7. And faithful witness i: 5; iii: 14; xix: 11. Please examine this subject:

TYPE. Now turn to Lev. xxiii: 10, 11; when you reap the harvest (in the spring,) then ye shall bring a sheaf of the first fruits, and the Priest shall wave it before the Lord—on the morrow after the Sabbath, (as in 3d v.). And ye shall count from the day after the Sabbath, (the some 7th day Sabbath in 3d v.) the day after ye offer the wave sheaf, 7 Sabbaths shall be complete; that is, counting the next day after the 7 Sabbaths, which will make 50 days, 16, 17 vs.; then with the sacrifices they are to offer two wave leaves, the bread made from the harvested grain; see 17-20. Now turn to Exo. xxxiv: 21, 22: here we see God required the people to keep the 7th day Sabbath, i. e. to rest in caring time, and harvest, but they were to observe the first fruits in their place, Deut. xvi: 9, shows where; begin to count the 50 days from the time thou beginnest to put the sickle to the corn. Now send the reapers forth the next morning after the Sabbath, what day is that? why, it is Sunday in the morning; so we see in the anti-type the morning of the resurrection instead of being a holy day (and as the world will have it the Sabbath) it was the day for the laborers to go out into the fields to reap the spring harvest. How could that be a holy day.

HYMN.—Tune—*Zion.*

By H. S. GURNEY.

Lo, an Angel *loud* proclaiming,
With the gospel of good news;
To every kindred, tongue and people;
Fear the Lord, give glory due;
     Proclamation,
Of the hour of judgment near.
Lo, another Angel follows,
With another solemn cry!
Babylon the *great* is fallen,
Peals like thunder through the sky:
     Let "Thy People,"
Now forsake her POIS'NOUS CREEDS.
Yet, a third and solemn message,
Now proclaims a *final doom*;
All who "worship *Beast* or *Image*;"
Soon shall drink the wrath of God:
     Without mixture,
Mercy, *now* no longer pleads.
Here are they, who now are waiting,
And have patience to endure;
While the DRAGON'S *hosts* are raging,
*Those* confide in God secure:
     Faith of Jesus;
And COMMANDMENTS, *keep* them pure.
Hear a voice from heav'n proclaiming,
"Write" the message, "firm decree":
Bless'd are they, who die in Jesus,
"From *henceforth*" forever be:
     The *Spirit* sanctions,
And the Saints ADORE HIS LAW.

# Footnotes

<u>1.</u>

Campbell translates this in three, and Matt. xxviii: 63, within three days.

<u>2.</u>

Small sea birds.

<u>3.</u>

Allow me, once more, to recommend to your careful, candid and prayerful attention, the simple, unadorned, scriptural, published visions of ELLEN G. HARMON, now WHITE. If you do not see the simple outlines of our history past *and at that time* in the future, marking our pathway, then I fear you will not comprehend what I have written. Reject it not because of her childhood and diseased bodily infirmities, and lack of worldly knowledge. God's manner has ever been to use the weak things of this world to confound the learned and mighty. I often feel to praise my God for this simple means to strengthen and encourage the little flock, just at the time that their teachers and shepherds were deserting them. It looks like God's work.

Milton Keynes UK
Ingram Content Group UK Ltd.
UKHW042108131124
451149UK00006B/700

9 789362 998736